MYTHOLOGIZING BLACK WOMEN

New Critical Viewpoints on Society Series
Edited by Joe R. Feagin

What Don't Kill Us Makes Us Stronger: African American Women and Suicide
   By Kamesha Spates (2014)

Latinos Facing Racism: Discrimination, Resistance, and Endurance
   By Joe Feagin & José A. Cobas (2014)

Mythologizing Black Women: Unveiling White Men's Deep Frame on Race and Gender
   By Brittany C. Slatton (2014)

Diverse Administrators in Peril: The New Indentured Class in Higher Education
   By Edna Chun and Alvin Evans (2011)

MYTHOLOGIZING BLACK WOMEN
Unveiling White Men's Deep Frame on Race and Gender

BRITTANY C. SLATTON

Paradigm Publishers
Boulder • London

All rights reserved. No part of this publication may be transmitted or reproduced in any media or form, including electronic, mechanical, photocopy, recording, or informational storage and retrieval systems, without the express written consent of the publisher.

Copyright © 2014 by Paradigm Publishers

Published in the United States by Paradigm Publishers, 5589 Arapahoe Avenue, Boulder, CO 80303 USA.

Paradigm Publishers is the trade name of Birkenkamp & Company, LLC, Dean Birkenkamp, President and Publisher.

Library of Congress Cataloging-in-Publication Data

Slatton, Brittany C.
  Mythologizing Black women : unveiling white men's deep frame on race and gender / Brittany C. Slatton.
    pages cm. — (New critical viewpoints on society series)
  Includes bibliographical references and index.
  ISBN 978-1-61205-049-2 (hardcover : alk. paper)
  ISBN 978-1-61205-050-8 (paperback : alk. paper)
  1. African American women—Social conditions. 2. Feminine beauty (Aesthetics)—United States. 3. Race discrimination—United States. I. Title.
  E185.86.S627 2013
  305.48'896073—dc23
                                                            2013008392

Printed and bound in the United States of America on acid-free paper that meets the standards of the American National Standard for Permanence of Paper for Printed Library Materials.

Designed and Typeset by Straight Creek Bookmakers.

18 17 16 15 14   1 2 3 4 5

Contents

I.	Introduction: White Men's Deep Frame of Black Women	1
II.	Physical Attraction and the Normative White Standard	37
III.	"Two Very Different Classes of Black Women": Race, Gender, Class, and Culture	59
IV.	Narratives of the Unwanted Woman	83
V.	Conclusion: The Disciplinary Power of the Deep Frame	107
References		*125*
Index		*132*
About the Author		*140*

◇

CHAPTER I

Introduction
White Men's Deep Frame of Black Women

> Just the term "black women" conjures up thoughts of an overweight dark-skinned loud poorly educated person with gold teeth yelling at somebody in public. I hope that doesn't make me racist but honestly that's the 1st thing I think of. (Lee)[1]

Lee, a middle-class white male with no black female friends and rare interactions with black families growing up, provides an automatic, highly racialized and gendered view of black women in contemporary society. Lee's quote sadly mirrors the views of many other white male respondents discussed in this book and disputes convenient notions that only a few uneducated, Southern bigots hold such strong, deep-seated views of black women. This book unveils provocative data on contemporary white men's perceptions of black women, capturing how black women have been socially constructed in racialized, gendered, and classed terms by influential white men historically and contemporarily. Perceptions of black women as hypersexual, unattractive (unless resembling a white aesthetic) welfare queens, and unworthy marriage candidates often represent the deeply entrenched perceptions of an everyday, average white male, who may be a school teacher, church member, company CEO, politician, or bus driver in our society. The deep framing of white men (and other groups in society) with white-created perceptions, thoughts, and emotions about black women guides how they interact and form relationships with black women. In brief, our *deep frame* is our deeply embedded world view. It guides how we think, emote, and process situations, and it often operates in an unconscious and commonsensical manner.[2] The deep frames of white men (and other racial groups) are often embedded with knowledge and information about black women (and other groups), created substantially by influential European men over the last several centuries. Deep framing is an important critical theoretical tool to interpret and explain the deeply entrenched perceptions and emotions white men hold toward black women, despite the fact that many have limited personal contact with them.

Possessing status, power, and control over hegemonic knowledge in society, white men, as opposed to other racial groups, are the focus of this book. White men have a vested interest in maintaining the status quo that places them at the top of race, gender, and class hierarchies, and white men have taken several measures to retain their power in society. One hundred thirty-four white males completed questionnaires for this book, of which over 48 percent are middle class and over 70 percent possess some college education or hold a bachelor's degree. Hence, these men are likely to hold positions of power and represent current or future leaders in society. The data in this book help to critically assess and elucidate white men's consistent exclusion of black women as relationship partners and problematize contemporary perceptions of a colorblind society.

Downplaying Race, Gender, and Class Oppression

Past and current studies on interracial marriage dynamics have provided problematic or nonexistent theories to explain the marriage trends between black women and white men. During the period of anti-interracial marriage legislation, Robert Merton and Kingsley Davis spearheaded the use of Caste Theory to explain interracial marriage statistics in the states that did not have a legal ban against such unions. Caste Theory argues that a white man did not have to marry a black woman, because her caste inequality allowed him to take sexual advantage of her (particularly during this period of legal segregation).[3] In 1967, Glen Elder used Exchange Theory to explain interracial marriage dynamics, which argues that women of lower social status use their attractiveness in exchange for marrying men of higher social status. These theories have long been the only explanations for the dearth of black-white interracial relationships; however, contemporary studies on interracial marriage dynamics find little evidence to support the continued use of Caste and Exchange Theories, and thus have debunked the relevance of these theories, concluding that people marry interracially based on compatibility, love, and personal choice.[4] Caste and Exchange Theories are indeed outdated methods, encompassing inadequate or insufficient theoretical explanations for interracial marriage trends and should be discredited;[5] however, interracial marriage theorists have generally debunked these theories without providing a critical alternative approach.[6] This may lead one to erroneously believe that the intersecting effects of race, gender, and class are severely reduced or have no impact on the decisions whites make regarding the type of relationship partners they choose, and that individuals make decisions about marriage partners, whether interracial or intraracial, based solely on compatibility, mutual goals, respect, and love.

Downplaying the intersection of race, gender, and class in interracial dating and marriage dynamics is a reflection of the broader field of mainstream social science. Often the types of theories or paradigms used by mainstream social scientists to explain racial dynamics (often the interplay of race, gender, and class is ignored altogether) obscure systemic processes, thus leading to conclusions that deemphasize racial oppression. The use of traditional concepts such as prejudice, stereotype, and bigotry place racism on a micro (individual) level and ignore how racism at the micro level is rooted in broad systemic or macro-level structures of racism.[7] Focusing on racism at the micro level often leads social scientists to assert inaccurate assumptions or conclusions, such as the notion that racism is declining. This faulty conclusion is a plausible one for mainstream social scientists because the constructs used to measure individual racism are usually a set of standard questions that do not change much over time. An example of a standard question might be "Are you against interracial marriage with blacks?" Whites responding to this question in today's society, influenced by political correctness and colorblind ideology, will often answer in a race neutral and colorblind fashion, buttressing notions of declining racial hostilities. The use of these outdated paradigms obscures the fact that racism is structural, nonstatic, and thus is changed and re-articulated over time.[8] These limited paradigms are unable to address the new articulations of racism and are widely used approaches because they often conform to and represent the ideology of "elite" white "decisionmakers."[9] Consistent with these white-constructed theoretical paradigms, mainstream social scientists rarely place whites as the subject or actor in creating and maintaining structural oppression, preferring to use passive terminology, and too often, racial oppression is presented in the past tense.[10]

Introduction 5

These problematic mainstream approaches support the hegemonic message that racial oppression, intersected with other elements of subjugation, is no longer of significant importance in society. In fact, a substantial proportion of whites today express that society is now a colorblind, level playing field. For example, using a large national sample, a recent study found that 36 percent of whites believe that America has already reached equality, whereas only 6 percent of blacks hold the same belief.[11] Additionally, a 2009 Gallup poll found that 82 percent of whites (including Hispanics) believe blacks have as good a chance as whites to get any job that they are qualified for.[12]

The work of contemporary critical scholars Picca and Feagin debunks the mainstream notion of the declining significance of race and the subsequent ushering in of a new colorblind society, by shedding light on the type of racial performances whites engage in while in certain settings. Their research analyzed the 9,000 incidents of racist events white college students reported in journals over a period of several months. Advancing Erving Goffman's research on frontstage and backstage performances, Picca and Feagin found in their study that whites know when and where to engage in racial performances, resulting in what they refer to as backstage racism. Backstage racism occurs when whites engage in racist and discriminatory racial performances in social settings or social spaces with other whites or people who appear white whom they typically feel comfortable with and by whom they have little fear of being reprimanded or "outed." However, when in the frontstage, around people of diverse racial and ethnic groups or other whites who will not tolerate such racism or with whom they are unfamiliar, these individuals will be more likely to engage in racial performances of colorblindness.[13] According to many analysts, strong racist and discriminatory attitudes of the past rarely exist anymore, if at all, based on quantitative polls that measure racial attitudes. However, research on backstage racism shows that much of those strong racist views still exist; they have just moved backstage as many whites have come to realize that expressing racist and discriminatory views in the frontstage is no longer socially acceptable.

Black Women's Exclusion

> Personally, [I] have yet to find any black woman to be perfect for me in my eyes. They have, on more than one occasion been rude, rather obnoxious, and generally lacking in formalities. In regard to appeal, they just don't do it. (Carlys)[14]

Carlys, another white male respondent in this study, also uses negative descriptors to define and exclude black women as relationship partners. His exclusion of black women is rather commonplace, as census data reveal that black women have the lowest interracial marriage rate of all women except white women. The percentage of black women in interracial marriages has increased minimally over the last several decades. In 1970, around 1 percent of black women were interracially married, and by 2000, this percentage increased to a mere 4.1 percent. Of the black women who are participating in interracial marriages, a large percentage of these marriages are of foreign-born, rather than American-born, black women. In contrast, other women of color intermarry at substantially higher rates, with 57.6 percent of American Indian women, 21.6 percent of Asians, 45.8 percent of Hawaiians, and 30.7 percent of Latinas in interracial marriages in 2000.[15] Black women thus have the lowest intermarriage rates of all racial groups of color.

Although black-white interracial marriage rates increased more swiftly in the 1990s and 2000s, they remain relatively low in comparison to the rates of whites with other racial groups.[16] The interracial marriage rate of black women with whites is much less than that of black men, with only 147,000 of the total 504,000 black-white non-Hispanic marriages in 2010 consisting of black women and white men.[17] From 1990 to 2000, black men across all education levels increased their intermarriage rate from 6 to 8.5 percentage points, whereas black women across all educational levels only increased their rate between 1.6 to 2.2 percentage points. Research typically shows that an increase in education has a propensity to lead to greater intermarriage rates; however, the data reveal that education does not result in a significant increase for blacks, specifically black women.[18] College-educated blacks, from middle-class backgrounds, are far more likely than other racial groups of color to be socially segregated from whites in residential neighborhoods and schools.[19] Additionally, black women do not have a high percentage of intermarriage with other men of color. White women, on the other hand, hold statistically significant intermarriage rates with men of all racial backgrounds. The 2000 census statistics show that interracial marriages involving white women made up 29 percent of all interracial marriages. These marriages consisted of white women married to "multiple-race" men at 12 percent, to "some other race men" (majority listed Hispanic as ethnicity) at 9 percent, and to black men at 8 percent.[20]

The census data illustrate a distinct and persistent trend over time: black women are not intermarrying at significant rates with white men (or men of other racial groups), and these marriages are not as positively influenced by education and class status as other forms of intermarriage with whites. A look at the literature on interracial dating trends and preferences also shows that black women (and blacks in general) are a severely excluded dating group. Much of the interracial dating literature analyzes the dating preferences of various racial groups, through examining the inclusion/exclusion of racial groups as dating options by participants on dating websites and newspaper advertisements. One recent study of interracial dating found that whites with conservative political views were open to interracial dating, yet not with blacks, as they overwhelmingly excluded blacks as dating options.[21] Another study by Phua and Kaufman found that blacks were the least preferred racial group and whites were the most preferred in personal Internet advertisements. The majority of the advertisers, across all racial backgrounds, "prefer either their own race or [w]hites, and least prefer [b]lacks, regardless of sexual orientation."[22]

Most significantly, a recent study by Feliciano, Robnett, and Golnaz found distinct gender differences in the online dating preferences of white men and women. White men are more likely to be open to dating outside of their race than white women, as white women tend to list a whites-only racial preference more often than men. Both white women and white men are highly likely to exclude blacks as a dating preference; however, white men are over two and a half times more likely to exclude black women than white women are to exclude black men. The study found that of the white men who specified a racial preference, 93 percent excluded black women, the most excluded racial group for white men.[23] Despite the fact that white men are more likely to date outside their race than white women and thus less likely to choose a racial preference in dating advertisements, their "openness" to interracial dating is largely exclusive to nonblack women.[24]

The Origins of White Men's Deep Frame of Black Women

The consistent exclusion of black women as relationship partners must be articulated from a critical perspective. The concept of deep frame is an important critical tool to understand and map the social and historical origins of contemporary white men's perceptions, thoughts, and relationship inclinations toward black women. According to cognitive scientists, a deep frame is our underlying world view and "conceptual infrastructure of the mind."[25] Our deep frames are strongly enmeshed and representative of our very identity, thus we often operate from it in an "unconscious and automatic" manner.[26] Our deep frames include cognitive thinking and reasoning skills; emotions; sounds; smells; and written, spoken, and visual discourses.[27] When we think, communicate, smell, see, hear, and engage in discourse, we activate our deep frames. Simultaneously racialized, gendered, and classed, our deep frames guide how we understand, perceive, and interpret society and groups of individuals occupying placement in each socially constructed hierarchical category.[28] Narratives are also central elements of our deep frames. Narrative stories are used to express principles, beliefs, values, and ideas. These stories include victims, villains, and heroes and are directly connected to strong emotions, such as anger, disdain, fear, anxiety, shame, and guilt.[29] The deep frames of contemporary white men (and other racial groups) are shaped by the social construction of knowledge and narratives forged by historic, influential, powerful white men over the past four centuries. These European men were explorers, travelers, colonists, thinkers, scientists, and physicians, such as Christopher Columbus, John Smith, Sir William Petty, Georges Cuvier, and Thomas Jefferson.[30]

These powerful white men socially constructed the culture and identity of what is now American society. Centrally, influential whites constructed the racial classifications of white and black, which, along with gender, class, and sexual orientation, directly correspond with who has privileges, accesses resources, and benefits most from various social institutions. The racialized terms of "white" and "black" developed as whites needed a system to define who was enslaveable and who was not during the burgeoning entrenchment of chattel slavery in the 1600s. Written into the slave codes between the years of 1680 and 1682, blacks became inexorably interchangeable with slaves and whites with freedom. The slave codes mandated that blacks receive different punishments than European indentured servants; blacks were not permitted to travel alone, be educated, own weapons, or own property.[31]

To justify these privileges, whites constructed themselves with positive characteristics and attributes, such as "industrious," "intelligent," "moral," "knowledgeable," "responsible," "law-abiding," "virtuous," and possessing an "enabling culture."[32] These positive descriptors mark the resources and benefits that whites have access to as natural and rooted in their savvy industriousness and "superior" nature, as opposed to being accrued through power and the domination of other groups. Conversely, whites constructed blacks as the opposite of white with myriad negative characterizations and attributes. The *Encyclopedia Britannica* entry in 1798 describes "Negroes" as follows:

> Negro ... a name given to a variety of human species who are entirely black, and are found in the torrid zone.... Vices the most notorious seem to be the portion of this unhappy race, idleness, treachery, revenge, cruelty, impudence, stealing, lying, profanity, debauchery, nastiness, and intemperance. ... They are strangers to every sentiment of compassion and are an awful example of the corruption of man when left to himself.[33]

The *Encyclopedia Britannica*, considered a well-respected source of "knowledge" and "information," provides a telling and illusionary social portrait of black bodies, which aided in reinforcing the belief of inherent black inferiority.

In addition, whites hierarchically ranked each racial group, placing whites as the pinnacle of superiority and blacks as utter inferiority, with other racial groups, such as Latinos, Asian Americans, and Native Americans, between those two polarities. This racial hierarchy legitimized slavery and provided economic and psychological benefits for whites by naturalizing whites' social position at the top of the economic, education, and cultural spheres during the slavery, Jim Crow, and post–Jim Crow eras. Influential historical figure Thomas Jefferson, in his 1785 book *Notes on the State of Virginia*, provides one of the earliest statements on the characteristics of blacks and the hierarchical arrangement of the races:

> Many millions of them [blacks] have been brought to, and born in America. Most of them indeed have been confined to tillage, to their own homes, and their own society: yet many have been so situated, that they might have availed themselves of the conversation of their masters; many have been brought up to the handicraft arts, and from that circumstance have always been associated with the whites. Some have been liberally educated, and all have lived in countries where the arts and sciences are cultivated to a considerable degree, and have had before their eyes samples of the best works from abroad. The Indians, with no advantages of this kind, will often carve figures on their pipes not destitute of design and merit. They will crayon out an animal, a plant, or a country, so as to prove the existence of a germ in their minds which only wants cultivation. They astonish you with strokes of the most sublime oratory; such as prove their reason and sentiment strong, their imagination glowing and elevated. But never yet could I find that a black had uttered a thought above the level of plain narration; never see even an elementary trait of painting or sculpture.... To our reproach it must be said, that though for a century and a half we have had under our eyes the races of black and of red men, they have never yet been viewed by us as subjects of natural history. Advance it therefore as a suspicion only, that the blacks, whether originally a distinct race, or made distinct by time and circumstances, are inferior to the whites in the endowments both of body and mind.[34]

Here, Jefferson's views on blacks as inferior to whites and Native Americans, grounds an early ideological framework of the ranking of the races and inscribes black bodies as biologically degenerate.

As with racial categories, white elites constructed intersecting class and gender hierarchies (as well as other categories such as heterosexuality), affording the most prestigious qualities and highest privileges to those in the dominant group of each socially constructed hierarchical category, that is, elite, white male heterosexuals. Elite white men constructed themselves as the apex of ideal manhood and white women as the height of womanhood in beauty and desirability, while defining black women as the lowest rung on the hierarchical ladder.

Early Framing of Black Women

Much of the early social construction or framing of black women is rooted in Europeans' first encounters with African women. In these first encounters, early images of black women were created, defining black women as the "other" and antithetical to European humanity and morality.[35] Early constructions of black women as animalistic and primitive were recorded in the writings of European travelers throughout Africa, as early as the fifteenth century. Most European travelers and scientists focused their analysis primarily on the Khoikhoi, a nomadic group derogatorily renamed the Hottentot, and the Khoison, a hunter-gatherer group, derogatorily renamed the Bushmen. Quickly Europeans generalized their beliefs of the Khoikhoi and Khoison as primitive and immoral to all black women.[36]

Khoikhoi women, most notably Saartjie Baartman, were examined and put on display for ogling European audiences, due to the shape and size of their buttocks. During Baartman's short life, she was displayed at Paris and London freak shows with an animal trainer, to show white

Introduction   13

audiences her "primitive" sexual body parts.[37] Baartman and other African women were dissected upon their deaths by renowned European scientist Georges Cuvier, to gather proof of their "primitive genitalia."[38] Every component of their bodies, including sexual organs, was deemed pathological and presented as evidence of their inferiority as a race. European scientists believed the "voluptuousness" of their bodies was proof of the overdevelopment of their sexual organs, their large buttocks a sign of their disfigurement, the narrow pelvis representative of the primitiveness of their "anatomical structure" and their place as a "lower race," and their vaginas a symbol of their primordial and insatiable "sexual appetites."[39]

Considerable analysis and research by these scientists focused on gathering evidence to prove the subspecies nature of black women, proving undeniably that black women were "as different from Europeans as the proverbial orangutan."[40] Through "science," black women became connected with innate animalism and were attributed with inborn animalistic qualities. Consider here Cuvier's use of multiple animal descriptors to describe Saartjie Baartman:

> Everyone who had been able to see her over the course of eighteen months ... could verify the enormous protuberance of her buttocks and the brutal appearance of her face.... Her movements had something of a brusqueness and unexpectedness, reminiscent of those of a monkey. In particular, she had a way of pushing out her lips in the same manner we have observed in the Orangutan.[41]

According to Sharpley-Whiting, this description of Baartman is parallel to how all African women were viewed by influential European thinkers, essentially as "the next of kin" to apes, monkeys, and orangutans.[42]

Rooted in this construction of bestiality, influential white men also defined black women as strong and masculine anti-women. European travelers in the 1600s and 1700s described black women in their journals as emotionally detached from the childbearing process, as strong and "brutish" enough to forgo rest after childbirth and resume their day-to-day business the very next day. In Edward Long's 1774 work, *The History of Jamaica*, he provides descriptions of African women bearing children with ease and little labor pain. Based on this belief, he purported that black women were unmarked with the "curse" of Eve, childbirth pain:

> Their women are delivered with little or no labour; they have therefore no more occasion for midwives, than the female oran-outang, or any other wild animal. A woman brings forth her child in a quarter of an hour.... Some have even been known to bring forth twins without a [s]hriek, or [s]cream; and it is [s]eldom they are confined above two ... or three days ... the negroes are persuaded that either the mother, the child, or one of the parents will die during the period of lying-in. Thus they seem exempted from the cur[s]e inflicted upon Eve and her daughters.[43]

This European framing of black women as strong and masculine with bestial reproductive capabilities and strength marked black women as "savage" and inherently different from Europeans.[44] It was used as evidence to justify black women's use as slaves, and enslavement was viewed as the only means by which to civilize black women.[45]

The physical appearance of many African women also marked them as intrinsically distinct from Europeans. Europeans defined women with white skin, a slim body figure, aquiline features, and a straight hair texture as the most beautiful, and ultimately the most feminine, women.[46] The white construction of beauty and thus femininity excluded black women because they "never become white."[47] Influential whites have long assessed black

Introduction **15**

women's beauty as inferior to whites. For example, Thomas Jefferson defined whites as having "superior beauty," stating the "fine mixtures of red and white" are "preferable to that eternal monotony ... that immovable veil of black."[48] Europeans made distinctions between black women with "African" features and those that were multiracial. Black women of full African descent were often defined as "thick-lipped" and "bullet-headed,"[49] whereas black women with white heritage were viewed as more attractive because of their white lineage and were sought after and paid for handsomely as sex slaves.[50]

Influential Europeans also quickly came to connect black women with animalistic, pathological sexuality, with French naturalist Georges-Louis Buffon and author Edward Long asserting in the mid-1700s that black women engaged in sexual copulation with apes.[51] Influential American leader and President Thomas Jefferson reiterated Buffon and Long's assertions of black female sexuality in his 1785 book *Notes on the State of Virginia*:

> Add to these, flowing hair, a more elegant symmetry of form, their own judgment in favour of the whites, declared by their preference of them, as uniformly as is the preference of the Oranootan for the black women over those of his own species.[52]

Here, Jefferson's deep frame of racialized and gendered knowledge of black women is already in action, as he has already learned and regurgitated derogatory notions about black women mating with orangutans expressed by Europeans before him.

As European scientists and physicians came to connect prostitution with black women, the construction of the sexually deviant black woman became a "fact" supported by "scientific evidence."[53] Research by Adrian Charpy helped to form this connection when, in 1870, he published an essay in a renowned French journal examining the similarity between the stretched labia of prostitutes and that of the Khoikhoi women, which had been ceremonially elongated—a tribal practice. With the work of Charpy and other European scientists and physicians, black women became succinctly and inextricably connected with prostitution and prostitution with black women.[54] Because of the racist work of European scientists, by the end of the 1800s, the definition of black women as innately immoral and sexually insatiable was a biological fact.[55]

Framing black women as sexual deviants allowed European men and later American slave owners to assert that black women could not be raped, that they were seductresses who gave their bodies freely to white men with no thought of impropriety. White men believed that this lascivious nature justified their sexual desires for black women, whom they constructed as subhuman, and allowed them to receive "uninhibited sex" from them that they could not request from "virtuous" white women.[56] Thomas Pierce Bailey describes this white desire for uninhibited sex with black women in his 1914 book *Race Orthodoxy in the South and Other Aspects of the Negro Question*:

> And the memory of antebellum concubinage and a tradition of animal satisfaction due to the average negro woman's highly developed animalism are factors still in operation. Not a few "respectable" white men have been heard to express physiological preference for negro women. If therefore animal appetite may become more powerful than race pride, it is not surprising that race hatred is superinduced upon those who offend against race purity; for abnormal sexuality easily develops brutality.... Thus the element of kindliness that often belongs to concubinage yields to a mere animal convenience that may be consistent with race enmity on the part of the white offender.... Thus does the negro woman become more and more a cheap convenience of the occasional sort, and the purity of the white race is protected at

the expense of the white man's appreciation of the negro woman's personality.[57]

Constructed as animalistic hypersexual jezebels, black women experienced mass institutional rape during slavery (and later during legal segregation).[58] Because they were not considered women or conferred the respect of humanity, black women were denied protection from assaults.

Post-Slavery Framing of Black Women

Mammy

With the culmination of the Civil War in the 1860s and the end of slavery, a new racial terrain was developing, and American whites sought to maintain their dominance and power by developing new knowledge and refashioning old, to define black women (and black peoples) and their subordinated place in society. To soothe the fears of a changing white America and nostalgically remember the antebellum South, whites developed the black mammy caricature. Mammy, the exact opposite of the lascivious black jezebel, provided imagery of trustworthy, respectable, and honest enslaved black women, melding characteristics of an ideal slave and an ideal woman within a patriarchal society.[59] Constructed as heavyset, unattractive, and with an asexual nontempting body—an inaccurate depiction— mammy knows her subordinated place and role and has "accepted her subordination."[60] She is the "ideal black female relationship to elite white male power."[61] According to bell hooks, mammy "epitomized the ultimate sexist-racist vision of ideal black womanhood—complete submission to the will of whites ... a mother figure who gave all ... who not only acknowledged her inferiority to whites but who loved them."[62] By constructing certain black women as mammies, influential whites create the ideal image of the duly subordinated black woman who will happily pass on to her children ideas of their proper subordinated places in a white society.[63] Mammy represents the ideal white constructed role for black women.

Strong Black Matriarchs

To justify black women's use as inexpensive laborers in an exploitative colonial system, Europeans constructed black women as strong, sturdy, and subhuman. Female bodies intrinsically born to "labor for others [whites] above them in the social hierarchy."[64] The strong, sturdy black woman construction was very useful for whites during slavery, making them ideal for exploitative labor, and post-slavery, it cemented their place as the proverbial domestic servant for white households. Whites also used this construction, post-slavery, to define black women as matriarchs—bad black mothers and wives—overstepping their bounds and hindering the success of black families. Social scientists in the 1960s, such as Daniel Moynihan, used the matriarch image to heavily criticize black women as pathological for taking the role of economic provider in the black family. These social scientists claimed that an exponential number of single black mothers existed, as a result of emasculating black women who, due to refusing to take on traditional gender roles, castrated black men, and caused them to abandon the family home.[65]

Constructing black women as emasculating matriarchs (and black men as too weak to lead) allowed whites to present blacks as the main cause for their economic and familial problems. Problems of poverty or single motherhood were the "failure [of blacks] to achieve normal complementary gender roles adequately."[66] Yet, whites ignored the systemically racist societal structure that greatly hindered or denied black men access to the paid labor force.[67] Hence, black women had to work outside the home and

Introduction **19**

take on nontraditional roles for family survival. Although much criticism was aimed at white women who worked outside of the home during this time, they were not labeled as matriarchs or masculine. Additionally, the concept of a black matriarch is problematic, because a matriarch assumes that a woman has "social and political power."[68] However, black women, both historically and presently, continue to be one of the most economically impoverished classes in society and exercise little to no political power.[69] The construction of the emasculating matriarch is a central narrative in the deep frames of many white men (and many people of color) and used to define black women as undesirable relationship partners.[70]

Baby Machines and Welfare Queens

The early framing of African women with bestial reproductive capacity and insatiable sexual appetite justified their use as slaves and human breeders. During slavery, with an economy dependent upon free black labor, black women's childbearing was considered beneficial and the reproduction of new black children was encouraged, as new slaves brought economic returns to white slave owners in an economy rooted in the slave trade.[71] In fact, white slave owners coerced enslaved black women to have more children through reduced work load incentives.[72]

After slavery, however, black women's construction as sexually libidinous with bestial reproduction no longer provided an economic benefit. With fears of an increasing population of blacks in the United States, and later the stagnated growth of the white population, influential white politicians used the already deeply entrenched construction of black women's pathological sex and reproduction to argue that black women were economically draining society with uncontrollable procreation and welfare use. During the 1950s and 1960s, white politicians and representatives framed black women's use of welfare as undeserved and rooted in poor family values and sexually licentious behavior. They constructed black women as proverbial leeches that usurped the welfare system by continuously bearing "illegitimate" children to collect welfare checks and avoid work. For example, Senator Wilbur Jolly cited "welfare dependence," illegitimate births, and "poverty" as a "Negro problem." He stated that "Negroes" and "'sexually delinquent individuals were increasing" in society at a much higher rate than the "virtuous members of society," whites.[73] Black women were defined as sexually immoral welfare queens, burdening taxpayers with their "tainted offspring."[74] Whites projected an array of negative attributes to potential black children. For example, one conservative politician described the "burden" of unborn black life in this way: "I do know that it's true that if you wanted to reduce crime, you could, if that were your sole purpose, you could abort every black baby in this country, and your crime rate would go down."[75]

Framing black women's reproduction as a threat, whites in positions of power took tedious measures to eliminate black women's procreative capacity, with some politicians proposing cash incentives for welfare recipients if they implanted Norplant, a temporary sterilization drug. Additionally, poor black women (and other women of color) were coerced to become permanently sterilized.[76] And in fact, 100,000 to 150,000 poor women, disproportionately black, were sterilized annually.[77] In many of these cases, black women were sterilized without their knowledge or consent.

Former president Ronald Reagan successfully used the narrative of the "black Chicago Welfare Queen" during his 1976 campaign.[78] He was successful with this narrative, as the framing of black women as sexually delinquent, economic welfare leeches was already firmly embedded in the deep frames of many whites. Hence, it was very easy for this narrative to have resonance for whites. The early

Introduction **21**

1950s framing of black women as immoral, sexual deviants, reproducing for financial gain, and its use by subsequent politicians, was the basis for the welfare reform act in the 1990s.[79]

It is also important to note that welfare in its inception was a white phenomenon. "Worthy" white women and widows with children were the early recipients of welfare—termed mother's pensions in the 1920s—while poor black mothers were excluded.[80] It was not until black women (and blacks in general) had more access to welfare in the 1950s and 1960s that the construction of welfare shifted from the worthy white woman, deserving of assistance, to the "immoral Black welfare queen."[81]

Contemporary Shifts in White Men's Deep Frames

During the eras of slavery and Jim Crow, American whites relied heavily on European constructions of black women as animalistic and biologically inferior. However, the civil rights movement and the subsequent post–Jim Crow era consisted of a shift, at least publicly, from explicit expressions of black biological inferiority toward that of black cultural inferiority. Nonetheless, research on backstage racism reveals that, in backstage settings, whites today continue to express beliefs of black biological inferiority. In this study, a small minority of white male respondents, approximately 5.5 percent, expressed a belief in the biological difference and inferiority of blacks. For example, a respondent alluded to that difference in the following quote:

> I am also a believer that people should stay with their own race. "[B]irds of a feather" thing. I am a scientist and believe that the white race is a subspecies of darker races. [A] microbiologist would not call a black colored microbe and

a white colored microbe the same species. There are more differences than skin color here. i.e., skeletal, musculature, stature, immune system etc. I do believe we were put on this world to procreate and to become one homogenous race. I don't want to be a part of that divine experiment.

This respondent (along with a minority of other white males in this study) reveals that old constructions of blacks as a biologically separate race are still operational segments of information in the deep frames of some white men, despite the fact that geneticists and evolutionary biologists have argued that humans have not been around long enough to form separate species.[82]

In present times, however, since the post–Jim Crow era and the societal shift toward political correctness and colorblindness, arguments about the subordinate status of blacks in society are primarily rooted in notions of black cultural depravity. The cultural depravity argument claims that blacks lack a hard work ethic, self-discipline, respect for learning, and conservative family values.[83] It is important to note that the denigration of black culture is not a new phenomenon; it has been consistent in the deep frames of whites for centuries, as many whites as far back as the 1600s have used the argument of black cultural inferiority, in conjunction with biological inferiority.[84] Nevertheless, this shift reflects the contemporary knowledge or segments of information in the deep frames of white men. The constructed knowledge says society is an equal, level-playing-field meritocracy in which race, gender, and class have no (or minimal) effects on one's life circumstances and that laws are generally fair and progress in society is based on merit, hard work, discipline, and the adoption of white-normed ideals and values. Thus, blacks are unsuccessful and black women are undesirable because they possess certain black cultural traits that are inferior. The majority of white male respondents in the study operated from this

Introduction **23**

lens. For example, a respondent stated the following about blacks and culture:

> I think that the black cultural identity of today is harmful to young black people because it emphasizes the differences between the black and white experience[s] in society and supports white condescension to blacks as fair and equal. Fifty years ago, special treatment was frowned upon, and separate treatment was obviously integrally unfair. The proposal that a man should be judged by his character and treated accordingly regardless of skin tone is now supplanted by the notion that a man's character (intelligence, ability what-have-you) is affected by his skin tone (through the treatment he and his progenitors received for his skin), and he should be helped to be made equal by special treatment. It is embarrassing to everyone involved.

This respondent, as with others in the study, places discrimination as an issue of the past and does not understand the need for redressing both past and present oppressive actions by whites against blacks (and other groups of color). He implies society should now be completely colorblind and governmental activity should remain neutral, which, of course, perpetuates whites' continued generational access to resources and power accrued through past and present discrimination. While strong notions of blacks as innately inferior and animalistic are still consistent, deeply enmeshed components in the deep frames of some white men, colorblindness and black cultural degeneracy offer a more tacit way to communicate negative views about blacks and to explain their subordinate status in society.

How White Men's Deep Frames Are Learned

Racialized, gendered, and classed knowledge constructed by influential European males over the last several centuries

24 *Chapter I*

is reflected within almost all aspects of American culture, and even many aspects of global culture; hence, it is continuously regenerated and learned by new generations of whites (and other groups). For example, even the concept of liberty, justice, and equality for all, embedded in the deep frames of whites, is not a neutral race-, gender-, and class-blind articulation. This country was built on genocide and the enslavement of people of color, patriarchy, and free enterprise. Hence, liberty, justice, and equality, when they were conceived, were for elite white males only and were never intended to fully include blacks (and other people of color), white women, and impoverished classes (among other groups). With constant repetition of verbal, written, and visual discourses this "knowledge" becomes embedded in a person's brain and is thus effortlessly learned.[85] Through parents, grandparents, other family members, television shows, news, movies, other media, the school system, and the Internet, this knowledge is consistently learned and expressed. And through these sources, white men (and whites in general) learn continually, whether implicitly or explicitly, myths about black women. In fact, 50 percent of the research respondents stated that they had been discouraged from dating black women by friends and family members (and some by black men). Consequently, many white men have strong views of black women, despite often having had limited experiences with them. White men may not consider themselves racist or sexist because their deep frames have normalized information about black women as commonsensical ideas. For example, one respondent (whom I will discuss in more detail in Chapter IV) stated the following diatribe about black women, yet claimed he was not racist:

> I rode a bus with black females (and black males). My interaction consisted of their Rude obnoxious behavior, their foul smell and their disproportionate and ugly bodies. This is

Introduction 25

not a racist statement because I do not judge people based on their race. My statements are my FACTUAL experiences.

This deep framing is very difficult to penetrate because it is so deeply embedded. It is not dismantled by a white male simply having a positive experience with a black woman or viewing positive images of black women in the media. Providing people with facts that refute their frames does not help in breaking down the existing elements because facts can be "assimilated into the brain only if there is a frame to make sense out of them."[86] Far too often white men's deep frames consist of negative knowledge of black women; hence, white men often do not have a deep frame of intrinsically positive facts and images about black women that would resonate in their minds with positive experiences with black women.

Individuals may not develop every component of constructed knowledge about black women. For some whites, their deep frames may comprise very strong racialized, gendered, and class components of blacks as innately and biologically inferior, whereas for other whites (as well as people of color), their deep frames may mainly consist of thoughts of black cultural inferiority.

White Male Respondents

This study used the Internet to reach a broad range of white men across age, region, and socioeconomic status in a backstage setting. Research shows that discussing "sensitive" subjects, such as race, could lead to socially desirable responses, whereby individuals provide the politically correct response. However, removing the interviewer and using self-administered questionnaires reduces the likelihood of this bias.[87] Because of the racial history of the United States and the present ideological move toward colorblindness, white male respondents may have been unlikely to disclose their honest views, thoughts, or behaviors in a face-to-face interview with a black female researcher. White male respondents also may have been unwilling to share their honest thoughts about black women with a white male interviewer that they perceived as having dissimilar views. In short, most people in society, particularly whites, do not want to be perceived as racists. Research, analyzing white responses to questions on interracial marriage and the intermixing of blacks and whites in schools and neighborhoods, revealed that whites were more likely to provide responses to black interviewers that were racially liberal, whereas their responses to white interviewers were more direct and not as racially liberal.[88]

Additionally, research by Picca and Feagin revealed how whites often engage in racial performances of colorblindness in frontstage settings, yet when in backstage settings (among other whites), they engage in racist behavior, including racial jokes and epithets.[89] Thus, in considering issues of social desirability bias and racial performances, open-ended online questionnaires as opposed to traditional face-to-face interviews were used in this study. The use of the in-depth online questionnaire is an innovative technique for analyzing the deep frames of white men, because the Internet acts as a backstage setting, allowing white men anonymity to reveal their deep frames of black women, which allows for more authentic information with a lower probability of social desirability. Online questionnaires have several additional advantages over paper questionnaires and face-to-face interviews.[90] Advertising the online questionnaire through a well-known Web-based advertisement site[91] allowed me to reach a wide audience of potential respondents from a variety of regions, ages, and professions.[92]

One hundred and thirty-four white males, ranging in age from eighteen to over fifty completed the in-depth online questionnaire. The respondents represented thirty-eight states and each region of the country. Forty-four percent of the respondents were from the South, 20 percent the Northeast, 24 percent the Midwest, and 12 percent the West. Respondents participating in the study were well representative of all age demographics, with 29 percent of respondents falling between the age range of eighteen and twenty-nine, 21 percent between age thirty and thirty-nine, 28 percent between age forty and forty-nine, and 23 percent age fifty and up. In terms of highest household income levels, 29 percent of participants had a household income that ranged between $30,000 and $49,999, and 19 percent had a household income that ranged between $70,000 and $99,999. Forty-two percent of participants had at least some college education, while 30 percent of respondents possessed a bachelor's degree.

A substantial percentage of respondents had no interactions or a minuscule amount of interactions with the black community, such as neighborhood composition and/or family interaction with black families growing up (see Table 1.1). A central component of this study was the type of experiences and interactions respondents had with black women, as detailed in Tables 1.2 and 1.3. I analyzed this information based on the number of close friendships respondents had with black women and their level of personal interactions with black women, ranging from no interactions to many interactions. Important here is that 38 percent of respondents listed having no close black female friends, while 31 percent reported having only one to two close black female friends (see Table 1.2). However, the concept of "friend" is of course very subjective. Respondents were also asked to detail the amount of personal interactions they had with black women. Seventeen percent of respondents admitted having had almost no personal interactions with black women, 29 percent listed having had few personal interactions, 31 percent stated they had had some personal interactions, and 23 percent listed having had many personal interactions with black

28 Chapter I

women (see Table 1.2). This question is also subjective, as some respondents may interpret saying hello to a coworker on a regular basis as having many personal interactions with black women, while others may not. Thus, a follow-up open-ended question asked respondents to detail the type of "personal interactions" they had had with black women. This follow-up response revealed that most respondents had service-sector, school, work, friend-of-friend, and other types of incidental socialization with black women as opposed to in-depth consistent personal interactions.

In terms of dating, 45 percent of respondents reported having dated black women, according to their definition of "dating," and a slightly larger percentage, 54 percent, reported having never dated black women. The high percentage of respondents who had dated black women, which is not representative of white men in society, is possibly

Table 1.1 Experiences with Black Community

Average Neighborhood Composition		Family Interactions with Black Families Growing Up	
No Black Families	35%		
A Few Black Families	55%	Never	24%
50% Black Families	8%	Rarely	48%
Other	3%	Often	23%
		Very Often	3%
		Other	2%

Table 1.2 Experiences with Black Women

Friendships with Black Women		Number of Personal Interactions with Black Women	
No Close Friendships	38%	Almost No Personal Interactions	17%
1–2 Close Friendships	31%		
3–4 Close Friendships	16%	Few Personal Interactions	29%
5 or More Close Friendships	15%	Some Personal Interactions	31%
		Many Personal Interactions	23%

due to their greater interest in the subject matter of this study, since participation in this research was based on self-selection. Moreover, individuals define dating in a variety of ways; hence, respondents who stated they had dated black women were asked to identify the types of dating relationships they generally had with black women, such as short term, long term, and sexual. Table 1.3 details the type of dating relationships respondents reported having with black women. The majority of respondents stated that they mostly had short-term and sexual relationships with black women, at 34 percent and 30 percent, respectively (see Table 1.3).

The fact that such a large percentage of respondents described themselves as having dated black women, which is subjective and can vary in intimacy, is an important element of this study to note, because this creates a bias toward participants who have dated black women. However, the participants who crossed the racial line of dating black women were often just as likely to have strong racialized, gendered, and classed views of black women as white men who had never dated black women; yet they often did not express those views as explicitly. This finding problematizes the argument that if white men simply "dated" or socialized more with black women their views would change. If a white man does not have a deep frame with positive perceptions, beliefs, and emotions concerning black women

Table 1.3 Types of "Dating" Relationships with Black Women

Short-Term Dating	34%
Sexual Relationships	30%
Long-Term Dating	14%
Long-Term Dating Leading to Marriage	0%
Other	20%

Note: "Other" refers to a combination of all relationships or friendship.

as a reference point, then he is unable to counteract the construction of black women as anti-hegemonic femininity.

Synopsis of Chapters

Chapter II analyzes the dominant discourse of "whiteness as normality" that respondents in this study consistently expressed. The discourse by the white male respondents often placed facial or body features, representative of a white norm, as the most desirable attributes. Chapter III assesses white male respondents' racialization of class and cultural expression. I discuss what one white male respondent coined as "two classes of black women," one that embraces "white culture," which white men viewed as higher class and more desirable, and another class that embraces "black culture," which they designated as lower class and undesirable. Chapter IV analyzes the central narratives white men utilize to explain or express racialized, gendered, and classed knowledge in their deep frames. The central narrative discussed in this chapter is the presentation of black women as the quintessential unwanted women. In the final chapter, I reconnect important findings with theory, making significant connections between white men's deep frames and Foucault's concept of disciplining behavior and actions. I discuss how the continuing negative construction of black women has negative implications on the relationships black women form with black men and other men of color.

Notes

1. In this quote Lee, a white male respondent in the study, responded to an open-ended question that asked him to "share any thoughts he had about black women."
2. George Lakoff, *Thinking Points: Communicating Our American Values and Vision* (New York: Farrar, Straus, and Giroux, 2006), p. 25; Joe R. Feagin, *White Racial Frame* (New York: Routledge, 2009).

Introduction   31

3. Kingsley Davis, "Intermarriage in Caste Society," *American Anthropologist* 43 (1941): 376–395.

4. Michael J. Rosenfeld, "A Critique of Exchange Theory in Mate Selection," *American Journal of Sociology* 110 (2005): 1284–1325; George Yancey and Sherelyn Yancey, "Interracial Dating: Evidence from Personal Advertisements," *Journal of Family Studies* 19 (1998): 334–348; Kristyan M. Kouri and Marcia Lasswell, "Black-White Marriages: Social Change and Intergenerational Mobility," *Marriage and Family Review* 19 (1993): 241–255; Ernest Porterfield, "Black-American Intermarriage in the United States," *Marriage and Family Review* 5 (1978): 17–34.

5. See Oliver C. Cox, *Race: A Study in Social Dynamics* (New York: Monthly Review Press, 1948), pp. 115, 123.

6. An exception is a study by Feliciano, Robnett, and Komaie on gendered racial exclusion in Internet dating. The authors posit that gendered racial formation theory, an extension of Omi and Winant's Racial Formation Theory, could be used to understand gendered racial exclusions in Internet dating. See Cynthia Feliciano, Belinda Robnett, and Golnaz Komaie, "Gendered Racial Exclusion among White Internet Daters," *Social Science Research* 38 (2008): 39–54. See Michael Omi and Howard Winant, *Racial Formation in the United States*, 2nd ed. (New York: Routledge, 1994).

7. Joe R. Feagin, *Racist America: Roots, Current Realities, and Future Reparations* (New York: Routledge, 2000); Feagin, *White Racial Frame*.

8. Eduardo Bonilla-Silva, "Rethinking Racism: Toward a Structural Interpretation," *American Sociological Review* 62 (1997): 465–480.

9. Feagin, *White Racial Frame*, p. 4.

10. Ibid.

11. Lawrence D. Bobo, "Laissez-Faire Racism, Racial Inequality, and the Role of the Social Sciences," in *Rethinking the Color Line: Readings in Race and Ethnicity*, ed. Charles Gallagher (New York: McGraw-Hill, 2009).

12. Frank Newport, "Little 'Obama Effect' on Views about Race Relations," Gallup, October 29, 2009, http://www.gallup.com/poll/123944/Little-Obama-Effect-Views-Race-Relations.aspx (retrieved March 31, 2011).

13. Leslie H. Picca and Joe R. Feagin, *Two-Faced Racism: Whites in the Backstage and Frontstage* (New York: Routledge, 2007).

14. In this quote, Carlys, a white male respondent in the study, responded to an open-ended question that asked him to "share any thoughts he had about black women."

15. Sharon M. Lee and Barry Edmonston, "New Marriages, New Families: U.S. Racial and Hispanic Intermarriage," *Population*

Reference Bureau 60 (2005): 1–40; Zhenchao Qian and Daniel T. Litcher, "Social Boundaries and Marital Assimilation: Interpreting Trends in Racial and Ethnic Intermarriage," *American Sociological Review* 72 (2007): 68–94.

16. Qian and Litcher, "Social Boundaries"; Lee and Edmonston, "New Marriages, New Families."

17. U.S. Bureau of the Census, Table FG4. Married Couple Family Groups, by Presence of Own Children/1 in Specific Age Groups, and Age, Earnings, Education, and Race and Hispanic Origin/2 of Both Spouses: 2010 (Washington, DC: U.S. Government Printing Office, 2010).

18. Qian and Litcher, "Social Boundaries."

19. John Iceland, Daniel H. Weinberg, and Erika Steinmetz, *Racial and Ethnic Residential Segregation in the United States: 1980–2000* (Washington, DC: U.S. Government Printing Office, 2002).

20. Lee and Edmonston, "New Marriages, New Families."

21. George Yancey, "Homogamy Over the Net: Using Internet Advertisements to Discover Who Interracially Dates," *Journal of Social and Personal Relationships* 24 (2007): 913–930.

22. Voon C. Phua and Gayle Kaufman, "The Crossroads of Race and Sexuality: Date Selection among Men in Internet 'Personal' Ads," *Journal of Family Issues* 24 (2005): 981–994.

23. Feliciano, Robnett, and Golnaz, "Gendered Racial Exclusion Among White Internet Daters."

24. See Feliciano, Robnett, and Komaie, "Gendered Racial Exclusion"; Phua and Kaufman, "The Crossroads of Race and Sexuality."

25. George Lakoff, *Whose Freedom? The Battle over America's Most Important Idea* (New York: Farrar, Straus, and Giroux, 2006), p. 12.

26. Lakoff, *Thinking Points*, p. 25.

27. Ibid.; Feagin, *White Racial Frame*.

28. Joe R. Feagin has been very influential in using the concept of framing to understand and articulate racial dynamics in society today. He developed the concept of the white racial frame. This concept has been influential in detailing whites' interpretations of society, themselves, and people of color, through a racialized perspective or framing. See Feagin, *Systemic Racism: A Theory of Oppression* (New York: Routledge, 2006); and *White Racial Frame*.

29. Lakoff, *Thinking Points*, p. 25; Feagin, *White Racial Frame*.

30. See Feagin, *White Racial Frame*.

31. Cheryl I. Harris, "Whiteness as Property," in *Critical Race Theory*, ed. Kimberle Crenshaw, Neil Gotanda, Gary Peller, and Kendall Thomas (New York: The New Press, 1995).

32. Kimberle Crenshaw, "Race, Reform, and Retrenchment: Transformation and Legitimation in Antidiscrimination Law," in *Critical*

Race Theory, ed. Kimberle Crenshaw, Neil Gotanda, Gary Peller, and Kendall Thomas (New York: The New Press, 1995), p. 113.

33. *Encyclopedia Britannica, or a Dictionary of Arts, Sciences, and Literature*, 3rd ed. (London: Archibald Constable and Company, 1798), p. 750.

34. Thomas Jefferson, *Notes on the State of Virginia*, ed. D. Waldstreicher (New York: Penguin Classics, [1785] 2002), pp. 146–150.

35. Sander L. Gilman, *Difference and Pathology: Stereotypes of Sexuality, Race, and Madness* (Ithaca, NY: Cornell University Press, 1985).

36. Beverly Guy-Sheftall, "The Body Politic: Black Female Sexuality and the Nineteenth-Century Euro-American Imagination," in *Skin Deep, Spirit Strong: The Black Female Body in American Culture*, ed. Kimberly Wallace-Sanders (Ann Arbor: University of Michigan Press, 2002); Ann Fausto-Sterling, "Gender, Race, and Nation: The Comparative Anatomy of 'Hottentot' Women in Europe, 1815–17," in *Skin Deep, Spirit Strong: The Black Female Body in American Culture*, ed. Kimberly Wallace-Sanders (Ann Arbor: University of Michigan Press, 2002).

37. Guy-Sheftall, "The Body Politic"; Fausto-Sterling, "Gender, Race, and Nation."

38. Gilman, *Difference and Pathology*, p. 85.

39. Ibid., pp. 85, 90.

40. Ibid., p. 89.

41. Tracy D. Sharpley-Whiting, *Sexualized Savages, Primal Fears, and Primitive Narratives in French* (Durham, NC: Duke University Press, 1999), p. 26.

42. Ibid., p. 24.

43. Edward Long, *The History of Jamaica, or, General Survey of the Antient and Modern State of That Island: With Reflections on Its Situation, Settlements, Inhabitants, Climate, Products, Commerce, Laws, and Government* (London: T. Lowndes, 1774), p. 380.

44. Jennifer L. Morgan, "'Some Could Suckle over Their Shoulder': Male Travelers, Female Bodies, and the Gendering of Racial Ideology, 1500–1770," in *Skin Deep, Spirit Strong: The Black Female Body in American Culture*, ed. Kimberly Wallace-Sanders (Ann Arbor: University of Michigan Press, 2002), pp. 37–65.

45. Ibid.

46. Patricia H. Collins, *Black Sexual Politics: African Americans, Gender, and the New Racism* (New York: Routledge, 2005).

47. Ibid., p. 194.

48. Jefferson, *Notes on the State of Virginia*, p. 176.

49. Solomon Northup, *Twelve Years a Slave* (New York: Miller, Orton, and Mulligan, 1855), p. 87.

50. Deborah G. White, *Ar'n't I a Woman? Female Slaves in the Plantation South* (New York: W.W. Norton and Company, 1985).
51. Gilman, *Difference and Pathology*; Morgan, "'Some Could Suckle over Their Shoulder."
52. Jefferson, *Notes on the State of Virginia*, p. 176.
53. During this time, much of the research considered as science or scientific fact was really pseudoscience.
54. Gilman, *Difference and Pathology*.
55. Evelyn M. Hammonds, "Toward a Genealogy of Black Female Sexuality: The Problematic of Silence," in *Feminist Genealogies, Colonial Legacies, Democratic Futures*, ed. M. Jacqui Alexander and Chandra Mohanty (New York: Routledge, 1997).
56. Guy-Sheftall, "The Body Politic," p. 25.
57. Thomas P. Bailey, *Race Orthodoxy in the South: And Other Aspects of the Negro Question* (New York: Neale Publishing Company, 1914), p. 43.
58. Hammonds, "Toward a Genealogy."
59. Deborah G. White, *Ar'n't I a Woman?*
60. Patricia H. Collins, *Black Feminist Thought: Knowledge, Consciousness, and the Politics of Empowerment*, 2nd ed. (New York: Routledge, 2000), p.73.
61. Ibid., p. 72.
62. bell hooks, *Ain't I a Woman: Black Women and Feminism* (Boston: South End Press, 1981), pp. 83–84
63. Collins, *Black Feminist Thought*.
64. Tamara Beauboeuf-Lafontant, "Keeping Up Appearances, Getting Fed Up: The Embodiment of Strength among African American Women," *Feminism, Race, Transnationalism* 5 (2005): 104–123.
65. hooks, *Ain't I a Woman*.
66. Collins, *Black Feminist Thought*, p. 183.
67. hooks, *Ain't I a Woman*.
68. Ibid., p. 72.
69. Ibid.
70. Ibid.
71. Dorothy Roberts, *Killing the Black Body: Race, Reproduction, and the Meaning of Liberty* (New York: Pantheon Books, 1997); Terri Kapsalis, "Mastering the Female Pelvis: Race and the Tools of Reproduction," in *Skin Deep, Spirit Strong: The Black Female Body in American Culture*, ed. Kimberly Wallace-Sanders (Ann Arbor: University of Michigan Press, 2002).
72. Kapsalis, "Mastering the Female Pelvis."
73. Susan L. Thomas, "Race, Gender, and Welfare Reform: The Antinatalist Response," *Journal of Black Studies* 28 (1998): 419–446.

74. Ibid.

75. Quote by William Bennett, a conservative commentator and former Education Secretary in the Reagan administration. See Robert Paul Reyes, "William Bennett: Abort Black Babies to Reduce Crime," *American Chronicle*, October 1, 2005, http://www.americanchronicle.com/articles/view/2685 (retrieved April 2, 2011).

76. Kapsalis, "Mastering the Female Pelvis."

77. This is the district court finding of the 1974 *Relf v. Weinberger* case. See Roberts, *Killing the Black Body*.

78. George Lakoff, *The Political Mind: Why You Can't Understand 21st Century American Politics with an 18th Century Brain* (New York: Penguin Group, 2008).

79. This reformative legislation culminated with the 1996 Personal Responsibility and Work Reconciliation Act, a welfare reform act under President Clinton's administration, which ended Aid to Families with Dependent Children (AFDC), capped welfare at five years and stipulated that welfare recipients find employment within a two-year period. See Roberts, *Killing the Black Body*; and Margaret L. Anderson and Howard F. Taylor, *Sociology: Understanding a Diverse Society*, 4th ed. (Belmont, CA: Thomson Wadsworth, 2008).

80. During the Progressive Era, reformers started a movement to provide mothers' pensions. Mothers' pensions benefited only 3 percent of black women. See Mimi Abramovitz, *Regulating the Lives of Women: Social Welfare Policy from Colonial Times to Present* (Boston: South End Press, 1996).

81. Roberts, *Killing the Black Body*, p. 207.

82. Joseph Graves, "Interview with Joseph Graves Jr., Evolutionary Biologist," *Race the Power of an Illusion*, 2003, http://www.pbs.org/race/000_About/002_04-background-01-06.htm (retrieved April 4, 2011).

83. Lakoff, 2006. *Whose Freedom? The Battle over America's Most Important Idea*; Crenshaw, "Race, Reform, and Retrenchment: Transformation and Legitimation in Antidiscrimination Law."

84. See Feagin, *White Racial Frame*.

85. Lakoff, *Whose Freedom?*

86. Ibid., p. 38.

87. Peter Kellner, "Can Online Polls Produce Accurate Findings?" *International Journal of Market Research* 46 (2004): 1; Seymour Sudman and Norman M. Bradburn, *Asking Questions: A Practical Guide to Questionnaire Design* (San Francisco: Josey-Bass, 1982).

88. Shirley Hatchett and Howard Schuman, "White Respondents and Race-of-Interviewer Effects," *Public Opinion Quarterly* 39 (1975): 523–528.

89. Picca and Feagin, *Two-Faced Racism*.

90. See Sean E. McCabe, "Comparison of Mail and Web Surveys in Collecting Illicit Drug Use Data: A Randomized Experiment," *Journal of Drug Education* 34 (2004): 61–73; Humphrey Taylor, "Does Internet Research Work? Comparing Electronic Survey Results with Telephone Surveys," *International Journal of Market Research* 42, 1 (2000): 51–63; Dhiraj Murthy, "Digital Ethnography: An Examination of the Use of New Technologies for Social Research," *Sociology* 42 (2008): 837–855; Nalita James and Hugh Busher, "Credibility, Authenticity and Voice: Dilemmas in Online Interviewing," *Qualitative Research* 6 (2006): 403–420.

91. This advertisement site is Craigslist, which is accessed by over 40 million individuals in the United States each month and posts advertisements in over 570 cities worldwide.

92. One of the criticisms of qualitative work is that it focuses on a very small subset of the population and is limited in generalizability. See Alan Bryman, *Social Research Methods*, 3rd ed. (New York: Oxford University Press, 2008). With this study, I sought to reach a wider, more diverse sample of white men.

◊

CHAPTER II

Physical Attraction and the Normative White Standard

Normalization becomes one of the great instruments of power at the end of the classical age. For the marks that once indicated status, privilege and affiliation were increasingly replaced—or at least supplemented—by a whole range of degrees of normality indicating membership of a homogenous social body but also playing a part in classification, hierarchization and the distribution of rank. In a sense, the power of normalization imposes homogeneity ... it is easy to understand how the power of the norm functions within a system of formal equality, since within a homogeneity that is the rule, the norm introduces, as a useful imperative and as a result of measurement, all the shading of individual differences.[1]

Entrenched within the deep frames of whites (and people of color) is the construction of whites and blacks as abject hierarchical polarities, with whites afforded positive imagery and blacks negative. Also embedded within the deep frames of whites is the normalization of whiteness, or the white norm. The white norm is an "unspoken form as a statement of the positive social norm, legitimating the continuing domination of those who do not meet it."[2] Whiteness, as it functions to wield power and maintain domination,

37

is made invisible and is deracialized because it has been solidly built into the definition of what normality is in society. Whites have essentially "'coloniz[ed]' the definition of normal" and have explicated difference, or opposition to this norm, as blackness.[3] As Foucault states in the opening quote, normalization is an instrument of power and plays a role in classification and hierarchization. Thus, the normative standard of whiteness continually reinscribes white as the ideal entity, as innate superiority, at the top of the hierarchy, and maintains white privileges and domination.

The social construction of whiteness as normality, and the obligatory standard, is central to how whites have framed society in racialized, gendered, and classed ways. The ways many whites see, understand, and analyze society and the people in it are rooted in an understanding and interpretation of society as defined by whites. Thus, white men's deep frame understanding of beauty, skin color, body features, facial features, and culture is from a perspective that is white defined and that privileges what whites have characterized as the epitome of beauty, desirability, and rightness.

In this chapter, I analyze the dominant discourse of whiteness as normality that white male respondents expressed in this study. White male respondents mark certain facial and body features as the most desirable attributes; however, these attributes often have a white norm. The respondents employ what I refer to as a discourse of comparisons. When sharing their thoughts on black women as attractive or as possible partners, they compare black women dyadically to the white beauty standard and judge black women's beauty based on their ability or inability to meet this standard. Those black women most capable of meeting the white norm—in body, facial features, skin color, and hair—are often considered the most desirable by respondents, whereas black women unable to meet these standards are perceived as less desirable. Some respondents reprimand black women to strive for this norm, while certain others view black women as genetically incapable of meeting it. The white norm is expressed explicitly by some respondents at times, such as white male respondents' expressing an interest in those black women who "act white" or "look white," whereas in other responses, whiteness is unspoken or tacit; for example, black women's bodies or facial features were described as abnormal. In analyzing and interpreting the responses and in understanding the dyadic and hierarchical nature of how western thought has been constructed, what goes unspoken as normal, is whiteness.

In most occasions, when respondents engage in a discourse of comparison, they use a white woman as the standard. However, at times, Latina and Asian American women are used to represent this norm as well, as these groups are seen as being closer to the white standard than blacks. As mentioned earlier, some Latinos/Latinas and Asian Americans are placed, by whites, above blacks and closer to whites along the white-to-black continuum.[4] According to Bonilla-Silva, certain Latinas/Latinos and Asian Americans are afforded by whites an honorary white status, because they are seen as having certain attributes that fall in line with white norms.[5] However, this classification is tenuous and always subject to change. An important point to note here is that often entrenched in the deep frames of whites is not only the "knowledge" of whites' superiority to blacks but also that other racial groups of color, including Latinas/Latinos, Asian Americans, and Native Americans, are superior to blacks, as blacks are placed the furthest from the white ideal.

Attraction to Black Women with "White Traits"

Around 54 percent of white male respondents describe themselves as physically attracted to black women, while

46 percent describe themselves as either rarely attracted to black women or not attracted to black women at all. Those respondents that describe themselves as rarely attracted or having no physical attraction to black women are most likely to define that lack of attraction to black women in the following language: "coarse" or "nappy" hair; "black" facial features, "big lips," and "wide noses"; dark skin; and "larger" and "disproportionate" body shapes. Those respondents that describe themselves as attracted to black women state that they are most attracted to black women's eyes, lips, and skin tone. However, some of the respondents that described themselves as attracted to black women state that they are not attracted to black women with kinky hair, wide noses, and large body shapes, and some have preferences for black women with light skin and straight hair. Although some respondents attempt to use "colorblind" language in describing physical attraction to black women, stating they find the same things physically attractive in black women as they do in white women and/or that they "see no color" when it comes to physical attraction or interest in women, it is important to critically analyze this. As the research discussed earlier shows, black women are overwhelmingly excluded as dating and marriage options by white men; thus, despite the profession by some white men of "colorblindness," the material reality shows that something else is in play.

As mentioned above, those respondents who find black women unattractive or that were rarely attracted to black women root that lack of attraction in those traits defined as "black": dark skin, hair texture, and facial features. In contrast, some respondents, including those who find black women attractive and those who do not, described black women with more "white" facial features and hair texture as the only attractive or most attractive black women, thus using a discourse of comparison in which whiteness is the standard black women's beauty is judged

Physical Attraction and the White Standard 41

against. Gilbert, a lower-middle-class Coloradoan in his thirties, describes himself as attracted to black women but of a particular type: "I am attracted to black women that fit my ideal petite body type and ones who are lighter skinned." His expression of being attracted to black women who are of a lighter skin color elicits the long-heralded notion that black is only beautiful when it is synonymous with a multiracial identity. Dillon, an upper-middle-class Texan over fifty, is more direct, stating, "I do find some black [women] attractive, but they tend to have more white physical features and are polished (good grooming, dress, athletic, professional). Alicia Keys comes to mind." Dillon specifically states that "white" features are what he believes make black women attractive and, like many other respondents, offered Alicia Keys, who is multiracial black and white, as the ideal black woman.

Ross, a middle-class white male in his forties, also from Texas, offers a similar standard of attraction for black women:

> Sexual attraction for me is a combination of physical and personal attributes. If I find a "black" woman attractive, it is because their hair type and facial features are more representative of the [C]aucasian race. If that aspect is attractive, then their speech and intelligence level would have to be more representative of that found more prevalent in other races (such as [C]aucasian or [A]sian—i.e.: anthropological mongoloids).

This respondent echoes a long historical message that only black women who look like white women can truly be attractive. Thus, he causally connects whiteness and beauty. Furthermore, he extends this to make a connection between whiteness and intelligence. Despite admitting to having no close black female friends and few personal interactions with black women, outside of work and church acquaintances, he places whites and Asian Americans as naturally more intelligent than blacks, with his assumption that intelligence is not as prevalent in blacks.

These respondents espoused white traits in black women as more beautiful, thus implying that multiracial black women are the most desirable. Indeed, there has been a long history of presenting black women with a multiracial background of white ancestry, formerly referred to with the derogatory term "mulatto," as the ideal and attractive black woman. During slavery, mulattos and quadroons, the products of nonconsensual sexual relations between enslaved black women and white slave owners (as well as overseers), were heavily sought after and paid for handsomely by white slave masters. One slave trader would not sell a mulatto child while she was young because he believed she could be of much greater worth to him when older, as a "fancy piece": "She was a beauty—a picture—a doll—one of the regular bloods—none of your thick-lipped, bullet-headed, cotton-picking niggers."[6] Although both multiracial and black women were enslaved and divested of rights, this quote clearly points to a distinction between the "beauty" and "worth" of blacks who were imbued with a white racial background versus the perceived "ugliness" of those blacks who were not.

Maxine Leeds Craig, in her work *Ain't I A Beauty Queen? Black Women, Beauty, and the Politics of Race*, traces the long historical trend of marking multiracial women as the "ideal type" black woman.[7] For example, in the early 1900s, the ideal black woman was of Egyptian type. According to the *New York Age*, this woman was defined as having

> A well balanced and symmetrical head, full slender neck, the features clear cut, with the appearance of being chiseled rather than cast; ... a fine Negro nose with a trace of the Egyptian and a slight aquiline curve; the mouth fairly small but well proportioned and a slightly pointed, round,

firm chin ... the marvelously fine curving eyelash of which the Negro race can be justly proud.[8]

Craig notes that this ideal black woman in the description above is of "mixed racial heritage" and although hair type and skin color were not explicitly stated, the desire for long hair and light skin was "so firmly established" that it "went without saying."[9] But most important here is that this quote is representative of the use of multiracial women as the "ideal representative" of the entire black race. This aesthetic is unachievable for most black women yet is supposed to be a symbol of their "finest expression," that of a white racial heritage.[10]

Davis, a lower-middle-class white male from Idaho in his twenties, outlines this notion of the beauty of the multiracial black woman. He describes what he believes an attractive black woman to be:

> There are some black women who are attractive. And they aren't full black. The only black women I find attractive are a mix of black and [E]uropean, black and [L]atino, or black and [A]sian. They end up with the tan complexion, and hair that doesn't look frizzled or like a [B]rillo pad.

Davis cites the racial hierarchy in his comments, essentially classifying only mixed-race black women as attractive: first Europeans, then Latinos, and then Asian Americans. Another respondent, Brock, a lower-middle-class Nebraskan in his thirties, also categorizes mixing with other racial groups, besides whites, as ideal. This respondent, who claimed to have many personal interactions with black women, including sexual relationships, states that "attractive black women tend to be slender with straighter hair and [A]sian-esque features." For both Davis and Brock, blackness must always be watered down with other racial groups for a black woman to be considered remotely attractive.

Black women, because they have been placed at the bottom of the race and gender hierarchy, are only beautiful based on their ability to look like brown-skinned white women or to appear the least black as possible.

Black Women with "Black Features"

Whites have constructed black features, including body shape, facial features, and hair, as the dyadic opposite of white features, a central component of the deep frames of many white men. Dating back to early European travelers in various African nations, whites have defined what they perceived as black features in negative terms. Because femininity is heavily rooted in women's physical body, what is defined as a beautiful body becomes the mark of femininity, and that beautiful body is rooted in a white woman norm.[11] The construction of "too-black" features as being "ugly" most significantly affects black women because being black, or as close to the spectrum of (white-defined) blackness, effectively locks black women outside of the definition of beauty, and thus outside of the confines of hegemonic femininity. This construction of beauty is firmly grounded in the deep frames of many whites (and many people of color) guiding how they see, understand, and make interpretations. Despite what many may perceive as changes in the overarching notions of beauty, meaning the acceptance of some black women, such as Beyoncé, as beauty icons, these changes are often surface level and have not uprooted the deep notions of black beauty as "at best less beautiful and at worst, ugly" in the deep frames of whites (and some people of color).[12] Thus, when asked about physical and sexual attraction to black women, white male respondents often view black women as outside of hegemonic beauty and femininity. Consider Bob, a middle-class respondent from Missouri over the age of fifty. He states,

Physical Attraction and the White Standard

I think black women's features are too extreme; they are too dark, and they usually are much too large for my tastes. The black women I have know[n] are very aggressive and have terrible attitudes.... The only black women I have found even marginally attractive are smaller, lighter-skinned black women with nice rear ends. ala Beyoncé.

Further, Bob states that he is most attracted to white women: "I think that white women's features are softer, yet more defined. I just think they are more attractive than women of other races." He describes white women as "intelligent, beautiful and confident," in contrast to black women. In fact, in several portions of his questionnaire, he describes black women as "very fat" and "very black" and attributes to them a host of other negative characterizations, such as "bad attitude," despite admittedly having very limited personal interactions and experiences with black women.

James, an older, college-educated respondent from Arkansas, who has had some personal experiences with black women, echoes Bob. When asked about his attraction to black women, he says, "Do not find attractive—facial features, hair, skin. Occasionally a black woman whose black features are less prominent will be attractive, but rarely. Most of the black women I find attractive ... are of mixed ethnicity and appear more white than black." For James, like many white male respondents, the less "black" black women look, the more attractive they become. Levi, a white male in his twenties from Tennessee, explains what he finds unattractive about black women:

> I'm not attracted to dark skin. Not attracted to the stereotypical hair or sometimes greasy looking hair and skin that [I] have seen enough on black women to associate with them. [I] wouldn't like it on other races either, but [I] tend not to notice it on them. [S]ome ethnic hairstyles [I] do not find flattering. [B]ut to each their own maybe some other guy finds it attractive.

Levi expresses that he is also not attracted to features associated with blackness, including skin color and hair. He notes that he tends to specifically notice these on black women and not other racial groups, which is not necessarily surprising because there tends to be a preoccupation among whites with blacks, more so than with other racial and ethnic groups. Throughout his questionnaire, he notes that friends and family would not be "thrilled" with his dating black women and that he feels social pressure from friends to avoid dating black women, stating that this is not out of hate on his friends' behalf but "mostly out of fear of being a pariah in the white community." When asked what would need to change for more white men to marry black women, he states, "Social pressure can dissipate, but being attracted to black women can't change." Thus, he seems to provide as a fact that although social pressure from friends and family may diminish, white men will generally never be attracted to black women, particularly black women with black traits. It is important to note here that often what white men view as attractive and unattractive is rooted in how society has been socially constructed in racialized, gendered, and classed terms, a construction that privileges whites and makes it appear commonsensical that blackness, including black facial features, dark skin, and hair texture, is unattractive.

Another respondent, Dan, an older, working-class male from the Midwest, plainly articulates one of the most racialized and gendered components of the construction of black female bodies: "I tend to read African features as somewhat masculine. The 'blacker' the person, the less femininity I tend to see." Whereas the other respondents allude to black or too-black features as a negative "extreme" that indicates unattractiveness, Dan articulates that perceived unattractiveness as a sign of masculinity. Dan's assertion that black features on black women are masculine is rooted in the deeply racialized and gendered construction of the black

Physical Attraction and the White Standard   47

female body, which includes the firm denial of femininity, beauty, and womanhood.

A recent study by Goff, Thomas, and Jackson on personal perceptions of attractiveness reveals how whites (and other racial groups) connect blackness with masculinity. In this study, a large sample of college students, predominantly white (82 percent) and male (72 percent), were shown several head shots of black women, black men, white women, and white men for a period of five seconds and then asked to judge the pictures in terms of perceived masculinity, femininity, and attractiveness, among other factors. Important findings of the study are that the predominantly white participants perceived black faces as more masculine than white faces, that participants had greater accuracy in guessing the gender of black men as opposed to black women, and white women as opposed to black women, and that participants perceived black men as slightly more attractive than white men, and white women as more attractive than black women. The participants often perceived black women (in the pictures) as being men and as less attractive than both black men and white women. The authors show the historical construction of blackness as masculine, as both black men and women were perceived as more masculine than white women and men, and black women were rated as "less attractive" based on their perceived masculinity according to the respondents.[13] This study shows how deeply the construction of black women as masculine is rooted in the racialized and gendered deep frames of many whites. Our deep frames often operate unconsciously, without people knowing it.[14] The construction of blackness (black woman) as masculine is often deeply ingrained in the white mind, thus, for Dan "blackness" automatically activates his deep frame, which informs him exactly what blackness is—masculine—irrespective of gender.

It is also important to note that the construction of black female bodies as the opposite of femininity was not just for the purposes defining the black women as masculine for the economic benefit of slavery, because black women's "strong" bodies could work the fields and bear children. They were also constructed as the opposite of femininity so that they would not be a legitimate source of competition for white women, and if they are masculine than they are not worthy, legitimate partners for white men (or even black men, for that matter). A black woman can be desired behind closed doors by white men or experience rare circumstances of outward affection, but in an open and legitimate sense, she is not an acknowledged body of competition to white women because she has been constructed as a body that does not compare.

The Black Sexual Body

Black women's physical and sexual body parts, particularly the buttocks and vagina, were a subject of complex thoughts among white male respondents. As with facial features, a discourse of racial comparison was utilized in which a white standard was directly or indirectly espoused in white men's statements on physical and sexual attraction to black women. Their discourse simultaneously presented black women's buttocks as a site of sexual/physical attraction and of condemnation. Drake, who is in his twenties and resides in Nevada, discusses his attraction for black women with larger buttocks:

> I am sexually attracted to most all women, but black women have a certain "exotic" look to them, and I like that. Specifically, I really love black women with bubble butts and nice legs, and who are fit.

This respondent, who was dating a black woman at the time of the study, describes himself as mostly attracted to nonwhite women, stating that he is "attracted to black and Latina women. They have beautiful skin and eyes. I also love that they have a generally fuller figure and more voluptuous. I like a nice bubble butt." Drake defines black women as "exotic," which may play a role in exciting his attraction to black women. Historically black women's buttocks have been an integral component in influential European men defining black women as having an "exotic," sexual body. Doug, a white male in his twenties who resides in Vermont, states, "I like big butts. In high school I read (and looked at) King magazine, which is like Maxim but for a black audience, and all the models have really big butts."

Black women's buttocks have long been a hallmark of white-defined black sexuality, with the "protruding" black butt representing "primitive," "raw," "uncivilized," and "heightened" sexuality, one that was historically denigrated and pathologized.[15] In today's commodity culture, the black butt has been recommoditized and is now popularized and more acceptable in mainstream white society. White men in contemporary times can more openly express their desire for full, black butts, and those white women (as well as women of other racial and ethnic groups) who do not possess a full behind can now attempt to recreate or emulate black women's butts through special clothing, fat injections, and other types of "booty-enhancing" techniques. Clothing companies financially capitalize on this new desire for the protruding black butt. Victoria Secret's creation of "uplift" jeans, which include a "built-in back panel" that "lifts" the buttocks up "from the inside, yet is completely invisible from the outside" is an example of this economic end.[16] Thus, black women's buttocks have entered mainstream white society as more acceptable and have been appropriated by whites as a symbol of "beauty," all while providing (as in the past) an economically rewarding commodity, one that white women and white men can now openly claim as desirable.

Nonetheless, the desire for black women's buttocks also comes with exceptions and stipulations, as so defined by whites. Not all white men have accepted the beauty of the black butt; for some, it is too visible a sign or a reminder of blackness. Additionally, there are stipulations for black women's buttocks. To be acceptable, the buttocks must be white-defined proportional; if not, it can be considered as pathological as it was during the days of Saartjie Baartman. Consider Morris, a middle-class male in his forties who resides in New Jersey; he states, "Black women tend to have larger hips and butts, which is often a turn-off for me. I like a girl's ass but not a big one. Sorry. I know lots of guys do." Although Morris is considerably tame in his response, others were not. Jean, a college-educated respondent in his forties residing in Delaware, describes black women's butts as "[h]uge, sloppy asses." Another respondent, twenty-year-old Quincy, an Ohioan, describes his aversion to black women's butts in this way, "Ghetto booty, no thank you."

Several white males expressed similar views by characterizing black women's buttocks, "curves," and bodies as being out of proportion and indicating that they find black women with "disproportionate" buttocks and shapes unattractive. Raymond, a forty-year-old respondent from Louisiana, states that "[s]ome black women have excellent figures that are well proportioned, but not most." Jay, a North Carolinian in his twenties, expresses that he finds "most things about black women attractive, except for ... a disproportionate 'rear end.'" Similarly, James, mentioned earlier in this chapter, declares that what he finds unattractive about black women, along with facial features, hair, and skin texture, is that black women's "rear ends are too large and out of proportion." Providing his take on proportional buttocks and black women, Nelson, a middle-class male in his twenties from Idaho, shares what he ideally looks for in women:

White in ethnicity, tan in complexion. Between 5'3 and 5'7 105 to 140 lbs. Hair color isn't really that important, although blonde is preferable. Breast and ass should be well proportioned to the rest of the body. Long hair is good. And blue or green or grey eyes.

When asked if he could find his ideal woman among black women, he states,

> I have yet to meet a black woman who is well proportioned and has a good personality. And for the most part, they don't have blue green or grey eyes.

He later states that "Beyoncé has an ass that is well proportioned to the rest of her body. Alicia Keys is very petite with gorgeous eyes. That is about as far as it goes with me being sexually attracted to black women." Similarly, Wallace, another respondent from Delaware, who is college educated, middle class and in his forties, describes himself as rarely attracted to black women, stating, "I think some normal weight black wom[e]n have nice above average breast and plump butts that [are] nice. Most black wom[e]n have fat butts and are ugly."

Black women's buttocks have been constructed as a site of sexual attraction, as noted earlier, because the protruding size emphasizes sexual licentiousness, yet at the same time a spectacle and pathology. Thus, although on the one hand several white males find the "black butt" attractive, both physically and sexually, others see it as a pathologized and racialized spectacle. Consider, for example, the white males' descriptors of black women's butts as too "fat," "sloppy," "ghetto," and disproportionate. The European creation of the "disease" steatopygia, which is defined as a high degree of fat in the buttocks, was used historically by white scientists to describe the "unnatural," "protrusion," and "disproportionate" shape of the buttocks of Saartjie Baartman and other African women as pathological, primitive, and sexually deviant.[17] Similarly, when white male respondents describe the black buttocks as disproportionate, they invoked these old historical constructions of the pathological black butt. Hence, in their deep frames, "proportionate" has a built-in white normative standard.

Likewise, when white male respondents mentioned the genitalia of black women, they almost always described it as unnatural. By defining black women's vaginas as deformed and unnatural, the respondents imply that what is normal is the genitalia of white women. Zack, who is in his twenties and resides in Nebraska, states that he is not sexually attracted to a "[p]ink vagina but dark skin around." Consider also Walter, a Coloradoan in his thirties, who provides a similar discourse: "[I] think their vagina is just not right looking, the black lips and the pink inside is just a total turn off." Walter expresses not only his lack of attraction to black women's vaginas but also the notion that the genitalia of black women are defected and abnormal. Extending this thought, Bob, a respondent mentioned earlier who expressed an aversion to black women, describing them as "very fat" and "very black," states, "I do not like to see black women naked because of their dark breast[s] and the black vagina area looks disgusting." Here again, black women's sexual body parts are described as a site of repulsiveness, rooted in the notion of their perceived deformity.

As with the buttocks, black women's vaginas have long been a site of pathology. Historically, the vaginas of black women have been used to oppressively mark them as primitive and as "evidence" of their innate inferiority to whites. For example, the "Hottentot Apron" of Saartjie Baartman, which was a "hypertrophy" of the labia, caused by "manipulation of the genitalia," was "diagnosed" by European scientists of the 1800s as a symbol of primitiveness and disease.[18] Pathologizing black women through the genitalia, Edward Turnipseed in 1868 made the argument that the black woman's hymen "is not in the entrance to the vagina, as in the white woman, but from one-and-a-half to two inches from its entrance in the interior."[19] Due to this believed "anatomical mark" of difference, Turnipseed deduced that "this may be one of the anatomical marks of the non-unity of the races."[20] Although the demarcation of difference and pathology regarding black women's genitalia may have changed over time from shape and formation in the 1800s to color scheme in 2010, it remains the same that black women's vaginas are constructed dyadically to those of white women. Thus, white men's deep frames of black women's bodies consistently and continually defines most anything akin to blackness as deformed and pathological.

Oppositional Discourse

In most cases, when a discourse of comparison was used by white male respondents, white women were the norm, or the standard, that black women were compared and judged against—their ability, or in most cases their inability, to meet this standard. In rarer circumstances, when a discourse of comparison was used by white males, black women were the standard, not white women, nor the achievement of a particular aesthetic akin to white women, such as fair skin, straight hair, and aquiline features. Those respondents who engage this oppositional discourse throughout the entirety of their questionnaire are more likely to have long-term dating relationships with black women, many personal interactions with black women, and to choose black women or Latina women as the women they are most attracted to. For example, Reginald, a North Carolinian in his twenties, states the following:

> Some things about trying to fit in to the "mold". I find that a black woman that accepts her beauty as a black woman,

> embracing her skin, hair, and form, is much more attractive than a black woman that tries to be a mass produced [B]eyoncé. Women in the mainstream that are more appealing to me are singers [E]rykah [B]adu and [I]ndia [A]rie, not the [B]eyoncé prototypes. Black women that learn to work with the incredible tools they have are much more attractive.

He goes on to say, when asked about his physical attraction to black women,

> body shape, skin tone, physical strength and beauty. [T]hey project beauty and strength more than white women, whom [I] feel, project more indecisiveness and immaturity with decisions.

Reginald, who described himself as most attracted to Latina women and who had been dating a black woman for the last three years, says that he finds black women and the various attributes of black women more attractive than white women. For most other white male respondents, black women who are considered beautiful (and the only black women a few respondents found even "remotely attractive") are the well-known singers Beyoncé and Alicia Keys. Both Beyoncé and Alicia Keys possess a white normative aesthetic; Beyoncé has a light brown complexion and wears her hair long, straightened, and blonde, while Alicia Keys, who is multiracial with a white mother and black father, boasts the aesthetics of fair skin, long and naturally wavy hair, and aquiline features. Beyoncé and Alicia Keys are placed in the mainstream media as two of the few representatives of "black beauty," and although they represent a multiracial aesthetic, they are still presented as a look that all black women should strive for. Reginald comments that he recognizes this particular "prototype" presented in the mainstream media. Yet in contrast to most other respondents, he appreciates black women who embrace their natural beauty and who do not manipulate it to appease white standards. Luke, a lower-middle-class Tennessean in his thirties, shares similar views on black women's beauty. When asked if he could find his ideal woman among black women, he stated,

> Absolutely. African traits are some of the "best" in my book. I like black women, mixed heritage or not, who prefer locks, braids, or short hair to artificially straight hair. Also, full lips and dark skin are blessings to be proud of. I have to be honest here and say that women of African ancestry are often not lacking in the hips and "booty" either as many from other backgrounds sometimes are a bit.

When asked about what he finds physically attractive about black women, he says,

> Do not: Like unnaturally straightened hair.... Do: Like very dark skin. Like kinky hair. LOVE locks on black women. Love African features such as full lips, strong frame, and beautiful dark eyes that pierce the soul.

Luke, who asserts that Latina women are those he is most attracted to, stated that he has had many personal interactions with black women, including having several black female friends and dating two black women. He, too, views black women's natural beauty as preferable to manufactured beauty that meets hegemonic ideas in society. He notes that black women should be proud of their natural features, commenting later in his questionnaire that black women should love themselves more. Unfortunately, accepting black beauty, for black women, is a difficult feat in a society subsumed by European beauty standards.

It is important to make a critical note here, however. Although only a small number of respondents considered darker skin, black features, hair textures, and styles as the most beautiful, this could be another form of exotification. In this sense, black women may only be beautiful in terms of how "different" or "ethnic" they appear and the "exotic" contrast that they can provide to whiteness. However, by analyzing the entirety of these respondents' questionnaires, it is hard to decipher if this was the case, as both Reginald and Luke do describe themselves as dating black women, being open to marrying black women, and surmising that it is likely that they will marry a black woman or a woman with "African ancestry" at some point in their lives.

Outside of providing an oppositional discourse of comparison, a few respondents did engage impartial language throughout the entirety of their questionnaires and seem to be genuinely open to black women and women of all racial backgrounds and did not uphold any particular standard of beauty, whether European or black. Larry, a working-class white male in his twenties from Oklahoma, responds this way:

> Black wom[e]n are unique in the fact that they are black women, but human is human. Attractiveness for me is not about race, but it is about personality and values. Be proud to be a black woman, but don't think that it makes you more or less attractive, to some it may be this way but to some it is not this way.

Larry states that, although he had rare interactions with blacks growing up and lived in neighborhoods with only a few black families, he has had many personal interactions with black women since adulthood and has dated one black woman, despite his family's disapproval of the relationship. In terms of the interracial relationship he was in, he shared that his "family is mostly racist, so sadly it was not taken well, but I let them know quick they were going to have to accept it." He noted "less racism" as one of the factors needing to change in order for more white men and black women to marry.

Chapter Summary

A critical analysis of white male respondents' physical and sexual attraction to black women reveals how respondents rank and compare black women's bodies using the white-constructed knowledge about black women and other racial groups in their deep frames. For many of the respondents, it is simply common sense, or fact, that white women are more attractive than black women, that straight hair is better than "kinky" hair, that light or white skin is preferable to dark, that aquiline features are preferable to full, flat, or wide features, and that black buttocks, body shapes, and vaginas are disproportionate or deformed. However, respondents' attraction to black women is also complex, revealing some of the recent flexibility in the prevailing standard of beauty. In contemporary society, fuller lips and fuller behinds are now more acceptable, and, in some instances, are considered beautiful. Yet, despite this complexity, whites, through appropriation and commoditization can control which features of the "other" will be considered beautiful and more acceptable, yet never with fear that it will elevate the black woman's beauty above their own. The data reveal that the old deep frame notions of black women, rooted in the racialized and gendered observations and interpretations of early European travelers, scientists, and writers, are still firmly rooted in the deep frames of many white men today. Although a few respondents expressed an attraction to black women who exemplified a black standard of beauty, this was rare. For the majority of respondents, their deep frames of racialized and gendered knowledge about black women shape their thoughts, perceptions, emotions, and what they define as beautiful.

Notes

1. Michel Foucault, *Discipline and Punish: The Birth of the Prison* (New York: Vintage Books, 1977), p. 184.
2. Kimberle Crenshaw, "Race, Reform, and Retrenchment: Transformation and Legitimation in Antidiscrimination Law," in *Critical Race Theory*, ed. Kimberle Crenshaw, Neil Gotanda, Gary Peller, and Kendall Thomas (New York: The New Press, 1995), p. 115.
3. Stephen N. Haymes, "White Culture and the Politics of Racial Difference," in *Multicultural Education, Critical Pedagogy and the Politics of Difference*, ed. Cristine E. Sleeter and Peter L. McLaren (Albany: State University of New York Press, 1995), p. 111.
4. Joe R. Feagin, *Racist America: Roots, Current Realities, and Future Reparations* (New York: Routledge, 2000).
5. Eduardo Bonilla-Silva, "From Bi-Racial to Tri-Racial: Towards a New System of Racial Stratification in the USA," *Ethnic and Racial Studies* 27 (2004): 931–950.
6. Solomon Northup, *Twelve Years a Slave* (New York: Miller, Orton, and Mulligan, 1855), p. 87.
7. Maxine L. Craig, *Ain't I a Beauty Queen? Black Women, Beauty, and the Politics of Race* (New York: Oxford University Press, 2002).
8. As Quoted in ibid., pp. 49–50.
9. Ibid., p. 50.
10. Ibid., p. 49.
11. Patricia H. Collins, *Black Sexual Politics: African Americans, Gender, and the New Racism* (New York: Routledge, 2005).
12. Ibid.
13. Phillip A. Goff, Margaret A. Thomas, and Matthew C. Jackson, "'Ain't I a Woman?': Towards an Intersectional Approach to Person Perception and Group-Based Harms," *Sex Roles* 59 (2008): 392–403.
14. George Lakoff, *Whose Freedom? The Battle over America's Most Important Idea* (New York: Farrar, Straus, and Giroux, 2006).
15. Collins, *Black Sexual Politics*; bell hooks, *Black Looks: Race and Representation* (Boston: South End Press, 1992).
16. Victoria's Secret, "Denim Sale," *Victoria's Secret*, December 2008, p. 28.
17. Sander L. Gilman, *Difference and Pathology: Stereotypes of Sexuality, Race, and Madness* (Ithaca, NY: Cornell University Press, 1985).
18. Ibid., p. 85.
19. Ibid., p. 89.
20. Ibid.

◊

CHAPTER III

"Two Very Different Classes of Black Women"
Race, Gender, Class, and Culture

> As long as the only standards of cultural acceptability continue to be those models of European heritage and upper-class white Americans, visible racial/ethnic groups will always be seen as inferior unless they adopt the cultural ways thought to be better. Black Americans as a group cannot claim parity, even relative parity, as long as their legacy is an African past and their adaptational reality is viewed as the lower-class, urban ghetto. The popular notion of "cultural deprivation" as a description of black ... children attests to a wholesale disregard of ... black life and culture. Individual blacks ... can escape only through the semipermeable societal membranes that Dubois referred to as "the Veil" but in doing so they must distance themselves from Blacks ... as a group both psychologically and culturally.[1]

By having control over hegemonic structures in society rooted in European imperialism, whites have monopolized, controlled, and defined hegemonic notions of culture within society. White-defined culture has been structured as having a direct connection to and being directly indicative of race, gender, and class. Thus, within the construction of culture is a notion of high and low, acceptable and unacceptable, which have direct implications on race, gender, and class politics. As whites have the power to predominantly control and influence what is considered knowledge in society, white cultural ideas and values are neutralized and normalized. White culture's "most formidable attribute is its ability to mask itself as a category," whereby whites may think of ethnic European groups, such as Italians, before "they think of their whiteness."[2] Central to the construction of white culture is the fact that it is naturalized as a "cultural marker against which otherness is defined" and the very existence of the culture of whiteness hinges on what it is not.[3] The power behind the neutrality of white culture is that it normalizes the exotification,[4] commoditization, and defamation of the "other," which reinforces difference and hierarchy.

According to McLaren, whiteness is the "invisible norm for how the dominant culture measures its own worth and civility."[5] Essentially, dominant culture is based on a white norm and, furthermore, what are defined as acceptable and ideal dominant cultural attributes are those believed to be expressed and fulfilled by whites. These cultural characteristics ascribed to whites include mastery of "standard English," the use of "proper" grammar, responsibility, respectability, work ethic, drive, studiousness, the delay of gratification (at least publicly), desire for education, and strong family values, among others. The construction of white culture is rooted in beliefs of whites as objective, "rational," "ordered," and "civilized," which is reliant on notions of black culture as "irrational," "disorder[ed]," and "uncivilized."[6] The perceived culture of blacks is seen as deviant and resistant to the norm. As Jones and Carter note, an African past and a present black culture constructed as "lower-class," inferior, and deprived will never be capable of reaching parity when the constructed norm for culture is rooted in a European ideal.[7] When aspects of black culture are deemed acceptable in society, it is because those aspects have been adopted by whites—who have the power to influence hegemonic ideas. Additionally, the adoption of black cultural aspects by whites often hinges on exotification and commoditization.

With the denigration of black culture, blacks are told and learn very quickly that they must adapt to the culture of the dominant group, and to successfully do that, they must distance themselves from blacks. Historically, it was widely believed that the nature of blacks made them inferior, and thus influential figures such as Jefferson viewed blacks as unassimilatable. In contemporary times, the issues related to black communities, such as continued poverty, are blamed on an "inadequate" black culture, with the underlying notion that if blacks only assimilated to the "proper" (white) cultural values and ideals, all their problems would go away. This notion is racialized and classed, as proper cultural values are deemed the adoption of white culture, while black culture, specifically what whites have projected on black culture, becomes synonymous with lower class and inferiority.

In this chapter, I analyze the racialized, gendered, and classed ways in which black female culture was discussed by the male respondents. Cultural difference was one of the central reasons listed by several white male respondents as to why they do not date black women. In particular, one male respondent articulated that there are "two very different classes of black women." He described one "class" of black women as those who "positively" embrace "normal" culture and the other class of black women as those who are enmeshed in "black culture" and all the perceived negativity that comes along with that cultural choice. Black women were viewed as overwhelmingly representing the latter. Central to this discourse on black women's cultural attributes is the use of narrative, complete with heroes, victims, and villains, by white male respondents to support their discourse. These narrative stories are central to their deep frames.

Black Culture and the Push for White Assimilation

When respondents discussed "black culture" and "behavior" in their questionnaire, it was often expressed in a totalizing fashion as problematic. Many respondents distinguish between black culture and normal behavior or a white/European culture. Important here is that black culture, in most all instances when discussed by respondents, was synonymous with negativity. Consider James, a respondent mentioned earlier in the text. He grew up in what he described as a very racist environment, stating that as a child he was "taught that blacks were terrible, nasty people that whites should not associate with at all." He now spends time working with black women in church and work settings; he shares the following thoughts on black women:

> The black women I have known, mostly in church and work settings, have generally been well educated, middle class, family oriented people. I have not found their personalities to be significantly different from white or other women I have known. They have all been fine individuals I have been glad to have as friends.... I think the black women I have known may not be representative of black women as a whole, but that is just an opinion.

James seems to provide a positive assertion of black women who are educated and family oriented, traits in this society that are generally associated with whites and white culture, as he asserts that these black women seem no different from the white women he knows. However, despite the fact that the majority of his personal experiences with black women have been through church attendance and teaching at a school with several black women, he provides a caveat, assuming that these positive attributes are not reflective of most black women. Later in his questionnaire, he explains why he would not marry a black woman:

> If I marry a woman I want to be part of her family, interact with family members closely. I would not want to do this with a black family. [I]t would also cause great problems with my family (not my children). There are many areas in which I am pleased to interact with persons of any ethnicity, but marriage is not one of them. I don't like many aspects of black culture, music, family structure, etc. Not necessarily wrong, just not for me. Some aspects of black culture are inferior.

In this statement, James makes it clear that he does not want to be a part of a black woman's family and friends; he says in another section of his questionnaire that "most white men" would agree with him on this. He connects this aversion to marriage and family with black women to black culture. For him, black culture is inferior, despite the fact that most of his personal experiences with black women have been with black women he deems as similar to white women. Yet, he still totalizes black culture as negative and substandard.

When asked about what would need to change for more white men to marry black women, James provides a classed image of black women, which he believes affects how black women are viewed as marriage partners:

> Well black women aren't gonna get any more attractive than they are now, physically. White men's attitudes toward black women would have to change. Also, the general image of a black woman as a baby machine, on welfare, poor, uneducated, whether truth or perception, would have to change. [U]pward movement of blacks in general in terms of education and income will make a difference.... This will likely lead to a slight increase in intermarriage. But I don't think it will ever be very high.

James declares as fact that black women will not become more attractive, and earlier in his questionnaire, he defines white women "as more physically attractive" than black women, claiming that both white and black men would agree with him on this. James presents a quintessential image of black women that is both negative and classed, although he does not necessarily purport this image to be representative of all black women. However, important here is that despite the fact that the majority of the personal interactions he has had with black women are with those in the middle class who are educated, the general image of black women that comes to his mind is someone who is "a baby machine, on welfare, poor, [and] uneducated." This image is rather pervasive in global mass media, because of limited positive media images of black women, and hence firmly rooted in the deep frames of white men.

"White Culture" as the Normative Standard

While expressing "black culture" and "behavior" as problematic, some respondents also implicitly and explicitly express "white culture" as the normative standard that black women should strive for. Roger, a middle-class male in his twenties from Minnesota, expresses this when he describes what he does and does not like about black women's behavior:

> I like the ones who live in the suburbs. Who are respectful of other people and who can keep their voices at an average level. Who dress like normal people. Who can speak proper [E]nglish. Who doesn't swear every other word. Who doesn't shake their necks when they talk. Black women can be beautiful as long as they act like a normal human being. I like their hair, when they straighten it.

Later in the questionnaire, when sharing his final thoughts on black women, he states,

> To me, there are two very different classes of black women. One is the more ghetto, loud, obnoxious group and the other is the normal human being group. I am not racist. I don't like people of any race that act like the stereotypical inner city black woman. There are plenty of black women out there who I would LOVE to have a relationship with. It has nothing to do with their race. It's an attitude thing.

Roger, who has no close black female friends, has few personal interactions with black women, has never dated a black woman, and lived in a neighborhood with no black families, shares rather strong views of what he likes about black women. Roger juxtaposes black women living in the suburbs as representative of a "normal human being" class and black women living in the inner city as representative of a "ghetto" class, hence distinguishing between a black class and a white class. Stephen Haymes's concepts in *Race, Culture, and the City* provide insight on Roger's comment. In his work, Haymes analyzes what Foucault refers to as "heterotopias," representative of "heterogeneous and relational spaces" that can be juxtaposed against one another and outlines how some spaces are constructed as "normal" and "ordered" at the expense of constructing others as "abnormal" and "disordered."[8] In this sense, urban cities are racialized, where "blackness is the urban Other," representative of disorder, danger, and abnormality.[9] Critically, Haymes notes that the residential spaces of blacks are racialized, which "transpose[s] racial identity, or stereotypical black images of disruptive behavior, attitudes, and values, on to residential location."[10] In this "racialization of social space," according to Susan Smith, "residential location is taken as an index of the attitudes, values, behavioral inclinations, and social norms of the kinds of people who are assumed to live in particular 'black' or 'white' inner city or suburban neighborhoods."[11] Thus, Roger racializes residential spaces, connecting positive attributes and norms to the spatial location of suburbia, a racialized space of "normal" white values, while he places negative attitudes and behavioral traits on the inner city, a racialized spatial location of abnormal and disorderly black cultural behavior. His discourse implies that if black women would only change their spatial location to a racialized white cultural area, they would also take on the proper white cultural values, attitudes, and behaviors. Roger's ideas, and similar ones offered by other respondents, reinforce the notion that the "problems experienced by black people are sharply bounded in space" and "when blacks live in the same geographical area, they produce social pathologies."[12] This belief ignores white power structures that create such racially segregated spaces.[13]

Another respondent, Gibson, who is in his twenties, is lower middle class, and resides in Wisconsin, also identifies a "white culture" as superior and representative of certain positive traits. When responding to whether he believes he can find his ideal woman among black women, he states,

> No, they usually have body shapes that I don't like (usually their butts are too big), and don't value education as much as white and Asian women. I have known a few black women who were raised around whites, and they don't have these traits.

Gibson has had very few personal interactions with black women and has lived in predominantly white neighborhoods. Although he states that he is rarely attracted to black women, he briefly dated a black woman, whom he described as being "raised around whites, so she mainly acts white (except for the horse hair)." Gibson's discourse makes a clear connection between a white cultural influence and the premium value placed on education. He later extends his comments by explicitly stating, "The blacks I know who were raised as whites are doing much better than blacks who are living in the black culture." Despite the fact that he describes himself as having limited personal experiences with blacks and describes the black women he has known as having what he perceived as white traits, he provides a totalizing image of black women (and blacks in general) as people who do not value education, an attribute he connects to a defunct black culture. Whereas Roger attempted to make whiteness invisible by subsuming whiteness in the categories of "normal human behavior" and "suburbia," Gibson very explicitly identifies being "raised around whites," thus a white culture, as a natural and factual embodiment of positive traits and ideals. His ability to explicitly identify a white culture is predicated on a comparison to what it is not, black culture. Gibson laments that, in order for more white men to be interested in marrying black women, "Blacks would have to stop living together in bad neighborhoods and start valuing education." In this quote, Gibson also locates a racialized residential space, while ignoring the role of entrenched racism that creates and maintains racially segregated neighborhoods. Discriminatory real estate and lending markets, redlining, and discrimination in the price of credit and interest rates make home ownership more difficult for blacks and create a forced concentration of black poverty in allocated residential areas with a concentration of poor public services, poor schooling, and poor real estate values.[14] Additionally, the black poor are the most isolated of all racial groups in poverty, as whites (as well as other racial groups) avoid purchasing homes or residing in areas that are "designated" as black.[15] Thus, Gibson's implication that blacks choose to live in isolated areas and can thus easily choose not to live there is a problematic viewpoint, but one that comes from his deep frame of white-constructed racialized and classed knowledge of black cultural degeneracy.

Caleb, a lower-middle-class male from Illinois in his twenties, also describes black culture as problematic. He feels he cannot find his ideal woman among black women: "All that I have met act in ways that I find repulsive." He extends this thought, stating,

> It is possible that a black woman from a different culture may act in a different way, which would make a big difference. I find the current trends in black culture repulsive.

Caleb is the only respondent to mention that a black woman with a "different" culture, possibly from another country, might have an acceptable black culture. As noted in Chapter I, of the black women married to white men, a large percentage are foreign born. Caleb, like several other respondents, explicitly states that he views the black American culture as problematic. Caleb has had very few personal interactions with black women but does describe himself as having two close female friends, one of which he admitted to having "casual sexual relations with." Although Caleb has a totalizing view of black women engaging in "repulsive" behavior and being from a "repulsive" culture and although he states he would never marry a black woman, he has had a sexual relationship with one. And he states that a sexual relationship is the type of relationship he would most likely seek with black women. Extending his thoughts on black culture and its effect on interracial relationships, when asked what would need to change for more white men to marry black women, Caleb says, "Black culture would have to change, and stop trying to be a separate entity. They would have to act more like a socialized American society." To Caleb, and other respondents, blacks purposely "separate" themselves from the broader society. He does not express an understanding that blacks historically and presently have been forced to be separate in society, both in an explicit and a de facto fashion. Thus, as a form of resistance, blacks, and black women in particular, have had to carve their own identities and safe spaces in society. In his assertion that black women would have to become better socialized Americans, Caleb, like Roger, also makes whiteness invisible, though it remains inherent in what "American" means to them.

Holding a similar view, Thomas, who is in his forties, middle class, and from Texas, also believes that he cannot find his ideal woman among black women:

> I find the "black" race to be, in general, morally corrupt as well as culturally and intellectually defunct. Unfortunately, other races have chosen to emulate the behavior of the black race vs. working to assimilate the black race into the common American, Euro-centric culture.

Thomas, relying on constructions of black intellectual and moral inferiority, explicitly names American culture as Eurocentric. Like the other respondents, he views black culture as problematic and places the solution to what he defined as the "defunct" and "corrupt" behavior of blacks in the assimilation of blacks to white culture. There has long been a "culture of poverty" argument espoused by white commentators and mainstream social scientists. The culture of poverty argument (directed at blacks) is rooted in the viewpoint that faulty values and behavior, commonly noted as immorality, broken families, delinquency, and a poor work ethic, as opposed to structural economic issues, are the root of poor blacks' problems. However, this inaccurate argument ignores "centuries of structural discrimination and socioeconomic factors" and instead places the blame solely on impoverished blacks.[16] Although this argument has predominantly been used to explain the culture of poor blacks, derogatorily termed the black "underclass," many of the respondents in this section used this notion of supposed bad cultural behavior and values of poor blacks to represent black culture in totality.

Norman, a college-educated male from Tennessee, also views black culture as problematic and white culture as the standard blacks must adopt. In the following quote, he states why it is problematic for black women to resist white culture:

> A culture that opposes "being white" and has fewer role model relationships results in more black women being constitutionally opposed to vulnerability and openness than women in other ethnic groups. I find this unattractive because it makes any romantic relationship less intimate by necessity. I find these traits equally unappealing in all women of all ethnic groups.

Norman views black women's denial of white culture as the root of their relationship problems, implying that being close to whiteness in terms of adapting to white culture, ideals, and values, is preferable. Through this "sincere fiction of the white self," which contains "deliberately constructed image[s] of what it means to be white,"[17] Norman extols whiteness as the catalyst for healthy relationships. By default, being black and the acceptance of black culture mean black women are less feminine: Here, the message seems to be that if black women accept white cultural values, which include soft femininity, they too could be desirable. Sincere white fictions are fundamental narratives in whites' deep frames, and these fictions are "sincere" because whites are often unaware of any alternative narrative.[18] In response to whether he thinks black women should have a strong racial identity today, he stated,

> Absolutely not. I think that feeling a need to be attached to a racial identity is an unnecessary and often burdensome restraint. In 1st, 2nd, and 3rd generation immigrants this is not the case because their grandparents' (e.g.) culture will still directly impact them. I do not feel any need to be boisterous because of my Irish heritage, any need to be nomadic because of my gypsy heritage, or any need to be punctual because of my German heritage. I am partly the

result of my family, of course, I am not bound to any code of "whiteness". People should be who they are, not who their skin dictates they should be.

For Norman as well as many other white respondents, racial identity is burdensome and seen as something that mainly people of color have or expressly want to hold on to. Whiteness is so normalized within society and American culture that many whites do not recognize it. When whites are asked to describe what it means to be white, research shows that a typical response is that they "have never before considered their white identity."[19] Thus, Norman can honestly believe that he is "not bound to any code of 'whiteness,'" even as he equates black women's opposition to white culture with their undesirable femininity, and thus their undesirability as a partner. That code of whiteness is built into most cultural components of society. Other racial and ethnic groups must embrace whiteness, and those groups that do not are viewed as not possessing desirable traits. Whiteness as power is so invisible in his deep frame that Norman does not even realize that as he denounced being bound to a code of whiteness, he directly engages whiteness as the norm to which black women must acquiesce. Whiteness is so normalized that he does not recognize that there could be any other alternative.

Burdensome Usurpers and Hardworking Bootstrappers

A central narrative used by some respondents is that of the burdensome usurper and the hardworking bootstrapper. Black women are represented as burdensome leeches juxtaposed against everyone else, meaning whites who achieve in life through hard work. This narrative is indicative of how black women have been constructed as welfare queens with uncontrollable reproduction, a central component in the deep frames of white men. For example, Greg, a college-educated, middle-class New Yorker in his thirties shares his thoughts on black women, juxtaposing the "good" from the "bad":

> In my experience, I have greatly enjoyed the relationships I've had with some wonderful women who have broken the stereotypes and just lived life the way they felt they wanted, instead of the way they felt they should. None of them trumpeted their differences, but still managed to stand out in my mind as exceptional individuals of innate grace and beauty. Not a single "ghetto-girl" or "fat black mammy" in the mix, though several may look that way from outward appearances alone.

In this statement, Greg implies that black women must prove their stereotypes wrong or work hard to not fit within the common stereotypes that, according to Greg, their physical looks seem to suggest. While these types of black women are fine, Greg juxtaposes them with black women who showcase ethnic difference and do not engage in proper American values and behaviors. He specifically describes what he does not like about black women:

> I dislike my dealings with the loud, abrasive, obnoxious, wanna-be ghetto or [A]frican-continental poseurs who make up for any real knowledge with a lousy attitude and in-your-face obscenity, especially in line at the grocery store. I dislike the ones who have multiple children on welfare by "father unknown," just so they can collect a check. I dislike the ones who name their children in an idiotic fashion (Tunisia, MGumbe, Propecia, Twandishia) just to seem like they know where Africa is on a map, or in a misguided attempt to seem more "African." They're Americans now, and need to grow up 10 percent. Individually, I look forward to further experiences with women of color who can step past

the media-fed role so many seem to fall into, and be useful productive members of society.

Later in the questionnaire, he shares his final thoughts on black women:

> Some black women that I have met are absolutely wonderful.... I know I've been blessed to come away from those meetings with incredible and unique friends. Still, even in the small town and rural settings that I am used to, I see a large number of black women, young and old, simply unable and unwilling to form relationships with men that last more than a few months to a few years.... I don't know the root of it, but I do see it as a major contributor to a continuing "state welfare" lifestyle where they believe they are entitled to a monthly paycheck, and all the trimmings, so long as they keep churning out children ... actual fathers are unnecessary. This needs to stop. I think at the heart of the matter, black women (as a whole, and in the media) need to stop seeing themselves as an oppressed minority, and look forward to building a future, one step at a time like everybody else, rather than expecting it to be done for them. I wish them luck, it's not easy, but it's doable.

In these statements, Greg provides myriad strong views about black women as undesirable. He espouses the central narrative of the burdensome, sexually deviant black woman, reproducing at will, and subsisting on government-rendered welfare checks. Welfare does not provide a comfortable form of living, and having more children does not result in a substantial gain in welfare funds. Greg describes black women as feeling entitled to a welfare check and even implied that welfare came with several benefits. This description of welfare is representative of how the limited funds of welfare have been severely taken out of proportion and reveals a lack of understanding of what living in poverty truly means. Welfare comes with no trimmings; families are just trying to subsist and survive. However, influential political figures, such as Ronald Reagan, have long created an illusionary image and discourse of black women living privileged lives on welfare checks. This welfare myth is an entrenched element in the deep frames of many white men.

Greg also lambasts black women for engaging in "bad" cultural etiquette by wanting to connect themselves with Africa and by giving their children names that are outside of the white normative standard. This is similar to other respondents who expressed annoyance at seeing blacks wearing t-shirts with African emblems or Puerto Ricans carrying Puerto Rican flags. He assumes that black ethnic names and anything akin to a distinctive nonwhite cultural identity is unnecessary and even foolish. As Regina Austin notes "uncommon" names bring about "hostility" among whites.[20] An important finding in this study is that white male respondents believed an American identity should come before any racial and ethnic identity. In fact, over 60 percent of respondents state that black women should not have a strong racial identity. For example, Davis, a respondent mentioned in the previous chapter, says,

> No. That would be like me saying that I need to stay in contact with my Italian heritage. I am an American. That is my heritage. Not what my ancestors did 7 generations ago. You don't see Irish people going around saying that they are Irish Americans. And they were treated like shit just like black people. There is black history month, where is the Native American History month? They need to get over it.

Blacks often assert a black identity as an act of resistance, borne out of a sense of "group solidarity" and "self-affirmation."[21] Thus, the disdain of a black identity, including ethnic names, is rooted not only in the normalization of white culture as superior but also in the need for whites to control other forms of cultural expression, particularly black cultural expression, which represents a symbol of black resistance and thus a threat to entrenched white-controlled power structures.

In addition, black women are not just told by whites to forgo a black identity and embrace a white cultural standard but are also often told that they no longer experience oppression in their lives. Greg explicitly advises black women to get over believing they are victims of oppression, concluding that this is the real root of their problems. His advice: simply stop believing you are oppressed, and you will not be oppressed anymore. This is a classic example of blaming the victim, whereby black women are blamed for their own oppression and are juxtaposed against whites, who live off merit, heed the American work ethic, and single-handedly bootstrap their way to the top without government assistance.

Andre, a college-educated Californian in his fifties, shares a similar narrative of bootstrapping white heroes, villainous black women who cheat the system, and taxpaying victims. Responding to whether he could find his ideal woman among black women, he states:

> In a few yes but [I] do not see black women as a whole being clean with a clean mouth instead of dirty talking all the time. I think most are uneducated and only want kids for welfare honestly [I] think the black race brings down the whole world and will always cost the world due to no education and 5th generation of welfare.

Andre has no close black female friends, has had rare interactions with black women, and his only interaction with a black woman was a sexual affair he had when he was young; yet he has deeply entrenched views of black women as welfare queens. He goes on to explain what he perceives as the difference between most black women (and blacks in general) and himself:

Some women really take care of themselves and get educated and like nice things but [I] feel that the most of the black race are too lazy to start at the bottom and work their way up as [I] had to do. [I]n all my schooling and diplomas [I] went to school with very few black men or women for they seem to like not being educated and living on the poor or welfare over and over with 5 kids and 4 dads.

Andre asserts strong views of black female bodies as sexually licentious and pathologically fertile and similar to the respondents mentioned earlier, he viewed most black women as welfare queens, a classed image. The welfare system that respondents like Andre refer to is no longer in existence; 1996 welfare reforms limited welfare to five years and stipulated that welfare recipients must find work within two years.[22] Thus, there is no longer a "state welfare lifestyle" or generational welfare to which these respondents are alluding. This example again shows the power of their deep frames. The 1996 welfare reforms have been in place for over ten years and have effectively eliminated generation-to-generation welfare subsistence; however, white men continue to view black women and welfare in the most derogatory and limited way.

Clearly, Andre believes black women have not developed a strong work ethic, unlike him, as he painted a clear picture of himself as the ideal bootstrapper who worked his way up from nothing. He stated that he noticed that he does not see black women at his institutions of education, yet he assumes that it is because of black negligence and lack of drive. As an older white male over fifty, he does not consider the historical and present discrimination that has hindered blacks from attending institutions of higher education. He also does not consider the fact that blacks often live in highly segregated neighborhoods and attend highly segregated and isolated secondary schools with poor funding and resources that often do not provide the educational training and background needed to be successful in post-secondary institutions.

With the strong framing of society in such a racialized, gendered, and classed manner, Andre, like other respondents, noted two different types of black women; he claims that some black women are educated, while others are lazy, and that the majority of black women fall into this latter category. Because of the lack of diverse media images and portrayals of black women, the fact that many white males have had few extensive and meaningful experiences with black women, and the way society has been socially constructed in a manner that places white power structures and dominance as normal, much of what these white men think of black women is derived directly from their deep frames of white-constructed knowledge. It is a racialized, gendered, and classed way of thinking, perceiving, and emoting that often results in white men having an image of a quintessential black woman with very little variance in their minds. Thus, lost is the fact that the numbers of black women seeking higher education at undergraduate, graduate, and professional levels are continually rising. Additionally, the *Small Business Administration Office of Advocacy Report* shows that, since 1997, black women have increased their entrepreneurial endeavors. In 2002, of all the black-owned employer firms, black women owned 29 percent, and of all the black nonemployer firms, black women owned 47 percent; in contrast, white women owned 17 percent and 39 percent, respectively.[23] These positive attributes and accomplishments of black women are often overlooked as white men attempt to make sense of black female bodies using a limited deep frame of reference.

Riley, an Ohioan and upper-middle-class respondent in his twenties, holds similar views as Greg and Andre. Responding to what would need to change for more white men to marry black women, Riley states, "Class and culture other than how terrible the white man treats the black. Get off your ass and work. Life is not some hip hop game where everyone is repressing you." Riley, who has had few personal interactions with black women and has never dated black women, similar to Greg and several other white male respondents, appears to view oppression as an excuse, and he reprimanded black women for being lazy; changing that behavior, assumedly, would increase the intermarriage rate between black women and white men. Riley also equated hip hop with black behavior; because of the commoditization of hip hop and its global popularity, it has come to limitedly represent black culture on the whole for some whites. Despite the fact that liberating and positive counter-hegemonic aspects of hip hop culture exist, these segments of hip hop do not get the same type of global mass media attention or production and hence the widely visible, mass-produced negative aspects of hip hop—such as sexualized black female bodies, misogyny, and phallus glorification—have come to provide an overarching and limited representation of black behavior and culture.

Understanding a Discriminatory History

Several of the white respondents in this chapter express a discourse that regards black culture as negative and problematic. Understanding black women and black culture through the lens of their deep frames, the perceived problems of black women are espoused as the ineptness of black culture. The class of black women who are "normal" contains those who do not trumpet ethnic difference and adopt white ideals and values. Whereas, the other class of black women contains societal burdens who have been unsuccessfully socialized and have fallen prey to a bad black culture. However, neither a bad black culture nor a

"Two Very Different Classes of Black Women" **79**

pathological culture of poverty impacts black women's lives; rather a pervasive system of white racism and discrimination does. Often, whites do not understand how whiteness has been normalized in the definition of what is right and proper, and often, they deny the historical and continuing effects of discrimination on the lives of black women. While many respondents fail to recognize this, a minority of respondents reveal an understanding of racial oppression. For example, Barry, a middle-class Ohioan in his twenties who described himself as having many interactions with black women, expressed a more critical take on discrimination and culture:

> They are the same as all other women inherently. However, in our [A]merican culture, due to slavery and an unfair segregation laws in the 60s, [A]frican [A]mericans have been forced to live in ghettos and this treatment still exists to this day. This means, that there are a large portion of African Americans who are still poor due to these circumstances of the past, and due to this, they have assumed a counter culture attitude and dress, also taken from popular media. Although they are inherently good people, they are more predominantly surrounded by poverty than their white counterpart therefore some people will have the view that black women are probably less committed, have sex at a young age, have many babies out of wed lock. This perception, I think, is due only relating to poor black women and not knowing enough educated black women who are identical to their white counterparts with the same education.

In his statement, Barry provides a critical overview of black women's experiences with racial discrimination. He does not discuss the impact of continuing discrimination today, such as the continued inequality in housing and education, and the disparity in black women's incomes to black men and white men and women, which makes survival a difficult process. However, he does distinctly recognize the impact of historical discrimination on the lives of blacks, including that blacks were "forced" to live in poor, isolated, urban areas, as opposed to choosing to live in "bad neighborhoods together," as mentioned by other respondents. Most importantly, Barry identifies the effect of poverty on black women's lives, as opposed to a defective black culture. Similarly, Reese provided an empathic understanding of the oppression black women have experienced:

> I think black women should have a healthy identity with their culture and stand proud for the unique journey that is specific to black Americans—a history that still has the scars of affliction and oppression, but continues to unfold through struggle and tears a great rising and overcoming. Black women have had a twofold struggle: that of being black and being black wom[e]n.

Like Brock, Reese does not discuss the oppression black women experience presently, and he does not identify the main source of that oppression, whites. However, he does reveal an understanding of black women's racial history and recognizes the importance of black pride and cultural identity. Unfortunately, Reese and Brock are in the minority, as only 6 of 134 respondents provide a general understanding of the discrimination black women experience, as opposed to placing blame on black culture, ignoring oppression altogether, or treating oppression as an issue of the past.

Chapter Summary

This chapter reveals that white men often have perceptions of black women as a monolithic lower class. Many respondents viewed the majority of black women as welfare users and baby machines. Even James, the older respondent who described himself as having most of his interactions with middle-class, educated black women, described his general image of black women as poor and on welfare. The power of white men's deep frames often leads them to make assertions about black women, despite personal experiences to the contrary.

Racialized, gendered, and classed notions of blacks are not the only segments of information in white men's deep frames. Whites also have a distinct image and knowledge source of other whites (as reflected by the respondents in this chapter). Their deep frames define whites with positive ideals, as respondents view themselves as having a "proper" culture, where they use the English language "correctly," work hard, do not use welfare, and give their children the "right" names. In contrast, many of these respondents view the majority of black women as adopting a negative black culture. Black problems, as well as other broader societal problems, have long been constructed by whites as being the consequences of a poor, degenerate black culture. Blacks are then reprimanded, by whites, to adopt the "positive" traits of white culture and to stop being burdens on society. Black women who adopt oppositional and resistant identities to a normative white culture are often denigrated because black opposition and resistance are threatening to normative white power structures.

Notes

1. James M. Jones and Robert T. Carter, "Racism and White Racial Identity: Merging Realities," in *Impacts of Racism on White Americans*, 2nd ed., ed. Benjamin P. Bowser and Raymond G. Hunt (Thousand Oaks, CA: Sage Publications, 1996), pp. 17–18.
2. Peter L. McLaren, *Critical Pedagogy and Predatory Culture: Oppositional Politics in a Post Modern Era* (New York: Routledge, 1995), p. 52.
3. Ibid., p. 50.
4. Ibid.
5. Ibid.

6. Stephen N. Haymes, *Race, Culture, and the City: A Pedagogy for Black Urban Struggle* (Albany: State University of New York Press, 1995), p. 44.
7. Jones and Carter, "Racism and White Racial Identity," pp. 17–18.
8. See Haymes, *Race, Culture, and the City*.
9. Ibid., p. 4.
10. Ibid., p. 8.
11. Ibid., p. 8.
12. Ibid., p.143.
13. Ibid.
14. Thomas Shapiro, *The Hidden Cost of Being African American: How Wealth Perpetuates Inequality* (New York: Oxford University Press, 2004).
15. Ibid.
16. Joe R. Feagin and Clairece B. Feagin, *Racial and Ethnic Relations*, 8th ed. (Upper Saddle River, NJ: Pearson Prentice Hall, 2008), p. 185.
17. Hernan Vera and Andrew M. Gordon, *Screen Saviors: Hollywood Fictions of Whiteness* (Lanham, MD: Rowman and Littlefield Publishers, Inc., 2003), p. 15.
18. Ibid.
19. Karyn D. McKinney, *Being White: Stories of Race and Racism* (New York: Routledge, 2005), p. 20.
20. Regina Austin, "Sapphire Bound," in *Critical Race Theory*, ed. Kimberle Crenshaw, Neil Gotanda, Gary Peller, and Kendall Thomas (New York: The New Press, 1995), p. 435.
21. Ibid., p. 435.
22. Margaret L. Anderson and Howard F. Taylor, *Sociology: Understanding a Diverse Society*, 4th ed. (Belmont, CA: Thomson Wadsworth, 2008).
23. Ying Lowrey, *Minorities in Business: A Demographic Review of Minority Business Ownership* (Washington, DC: U.S. Small Business Research Administration, 2007).

Chapter IV

Narratives of the Unwanted Woman

> The dominant group creates its own stories.... The stories or narratives told by the ingroup remind it of its identity in relation to outgroups, and provide it with a form of shared reality in which its own superior position is seen as natural.[1]

The global overarching construction of black women as the anti-woman[2] in beauty, sexual morality, femininity, and womanhood has persisted for centuries through pervasive racialized and gendered narratives (or stories) shared discursively, generation to generation, by whites. According to Delgado, the dominant group uses narratives to not only assert their superior position in society but also to define the subordinated status and position of subjugated groups as natural. The narratives created by rank-and-file white men about black women include the controlling myths of the black jezebel, sapphire, welfare queen, matriarch, and mammy.[3] While whites created narratives of themselves as "industrious," "intelligent," "moral," "knowledgeable," "responsible," "law-abiding," "virtuous," and possessing of an "enabling culture,"[4] these white-constructed narratives of both black women and whites are deeply embedded in the fabric of society and central to the deep frames of contemporary white men (and people in general), guiding how individuals understand, interpret, and perceive black women and whites.

The Narratives White Men Tell

As noted earlier, the majority of respondents in this study had limited personal interactions with black women and the black community. Ninety percent of respondents lived in neighborhoods with either no or just a few black families. Seventy-two percent never or rarely had interactions with black families growing up. Forty-six percent stated they had no or few interactions with black women, while 31 percent had some personal interactions with black women. Service-sector, friend of friend, and work interactions represented the most common contact white respondents had with black women. Only a small percentage of white men had consistent in-depth, meaningful interactions.

Strong racialized and gendered perceptions of black women as anti-women were most prevalent among respondents with limited personal interactions with black women and the black community—a substantial proportion of the research sample. As illustrated by my study, actual experiences with black women are unnecessary, as white men rely on old historically constructed narratives to understand and interpret black women. Contemporary white men learn these narratives from family, media, politics, and books, recreating and passing these stories on without reflection or analysis. Note here this response from Mark, a Michigan respondent in his twenties:

> Black women are like black people, which are different tha[n] white people. This is not a racist comment (doesn't that sound defensive?) we are just different socially, morally, physically ... etc. This does not mean one is better

Narratives of the Unwanted Woman 85

than the other, just different. I think most of us are attracted to those who share similar values, thus I am attracted to white women. Black women generally have different morals, values and social etiquette than white women, and I don't find the differences exemplified by black women attractive.

Mark has no personal interactions with black women, no close black female friends, and no family interactions with blacks growing up. His only interactions have been through service-sector experiences, such as ordering fast food at restaurants. Mark is very tactful and careful in his response to steer from using overtly inflammatory language, and he even provides a disclaimer that his comment was not racist, a disclaimer used often by respondents. However, his point is still clear, that black women are "different" from white women, and whereas white women excel in morality, it is implied that black women do not. Responding to why he believes the intermarriage rate is low between black women and white men, Mark states, "White men have preferences that aren't found in black women." In this perspective, black women essentially do not and could not possess what a white man wants or desires.

George, who is upper middle class, over fifty, and from Vermont, also expresses notions, though somewhat more explicitly, of black women having "negative" or "different" qualities from white women. When asked if there are any traits that predominantly represent black women, he stated, "Yes. Lethargy, poor speaking habits, little control of basic instincts." He went on to say,

> From my observations, black women GENERALLY are larger figured, more lethargic in their movements, and seem to lack incentive. Notice that I stress GENERALLY.... I am not a bigot, but this is the way it appears to me. Perhaps if I had more exposure to black women, I would see this differently.

George, similar to Mark, has had very little experience with black women, has no close black female friends, and has had few personal interactions, although he did date a black woman "briefly"; he also states that he is not open to marrying black women. Clearly, George has negative perceptions of black women, as he relies on conventional constructions of wild, unrestrained black bodies. Consider the similarities between George's comments and Thomas Jefferson's assertions in his 1785 work *Notes on the State of Virginia*. According to Jefferson, blacks' existence is based more on "sensation than reflection" and blacks have no "foresight," but only "sensation" and "desire."[5] George openly admits to having very few experiences and little exposure to black women, yet he holds strong views with no real material basis. George's comments, as well as other respondents' in my research, reveal how white-constructed racialized and gendered narratives about black women are deeply embedded in the minds of many white males, despite lack of interactions with black women.

Lee, mentioned at the beginning of this book, a Floridian in his thirties who has had few interactions with black women as well, describes what comes to mind when he thinks of black women:

> Just the term "black women" conjures up thoughts of an overweight darkskinned loud poorly educated person with gold teeth yelling at somebody in public. I hope that doesn't make me racist but honestly that's the 1st thing I think of.

Like other respondents, Lee attempts to soften his narrative of black women by offering an "I'm not trying to be racist" disclaimer. However, he expressed strong negative views of black women, despite the fact that he, like previously mentioned respondents, has had very few experiences with them. Lee has no black female friends, had rare interactions with black families growing up, and most of his interactions with black women consisted of work-related experiences and "drunken sex with a gal from Liberia a few times but that's about it." In this case, the term "black women" activated Lee's deep frame of negative images, thoughts, and probably even emotions about black women. Lee's quote emphasizes that the black woman conjured in his mind is dark skinned, and dark skin has been paramount with unattractiveness and inferiority in this society. His description is also classed, as he conjured up an image of a black woman with gold teeth, which may be more likely worn by individuals in the lower class. Despite the negative imaging and thoughts of black women, Lee admitted that he has had rare experiences with black women, which is evidence of how his deep frame of one-dimensional racialized, gendered, and classed knowledge acts as the sole reference for his perspectives. His only personal experience with black women was "drunken sex." As with other respondents, Lee may have negative views of black women, but that did not stop him from having sexual relations with them, an integral point that I discuss in more detail in a later section of this chapter.

Randy, a graduate school–educated white male in his thirties who resides in Tennessee, expresses explicit racist and sexist ideas about black women. He states the following when describing the type of interactions he has had with black women:

> I rode a bus with black females (and black males). My interaction consisted of their Rude obnoxious behavior, their foul smell and their disproportionate and ugly bodies. This is not a racist statement because I do not judge people based on their race. My statements are my FACTUAL experiences.

Later, when asked if he could find his ideal woman among black women, he states,

No! 1) smell—a natural musky animal smell that is foul and repulsive 2) lack of bathing on their part, BAD HYGIENE 3) disproportionate bodies, like some sort of mutants, stove pipe noses, grossly obese or disproportionate bodies 4) bad attitude, nasty in-your-face, neck breaking argumentative nasty attitude, the inability to show compassion or care about others, cultural inferiority teaches them the only thing that matters are themselves. 5) the female negro is completely lacking in any semblance of femininity (at least all those I have run into) 6) their HIV/AIDS as well as other STD rates of disease is 10 times that of whites! that's a CDC FACT ... check it out before dismissing it!

Aside from his experience riding a bus, Randy describes himself as having few personal interactions with black women and no close black female friends. Astoundingly, Randy, as with other respondents, prefaces his comments with a not-racist clause. Many whites recognize that contemporary society espouses a "colorblind" ideology—in name only—and a strong emphasis on "politically correct" language. This outward ideological shift has left some whites, as illustrated by several in my study, angry over their inability to openly convey their true beliefs about blacks, often rooted in old racist ideas of biological inferiority that they believe to be true.

Randy relies on historically constructed narratives of black women as naturally inferior. In comparison to European scientists of the 1800s, Randy marks the black female body as a site of sexually transmitted disease. European scientists of the 1800s and 1900s created a racialized link between the skin color of blacks and syphilis, believing dark skin a sign of leprosy and leprosy a form of syphilis.[6] This "scientific fact" (at the time) was further exacerbated by the connection of prostitutes with disease and black women with prostitution, which inextricably defined black female bodies as the embodiment of unbridled sexuality and disease.[7] Randy's projection of HIV on black women reflects historical notions of diseased black bodies and directly links black women with hypersexuality. Severely, Randy compares black women to animals. He extends this comparison when later in the questionnaire he states the "evolution of the black women into something that resembled a human being" is the only way more white men would marry black women.

Lyle, a respondent in his fifties also from Tennessee, follows this same racist and sexist logic. Like Randy, he states that he has had almost no personal interactions with black women, although he described himself as being raised by a "colored maid." In describing his attraction to black women, he states, "I have no more attraction to them than I would to any primate. They do not strike me as truly evolved humanity." He continues this line of reasoning when he responds to what would need to change for more white men to marry black women: "Some form of mass insanity or a disease which killed all [A]sian, [C]aucasian and [H]ispanic women. It would have to decimate the sheep population too." Lyle, relying heavily on old white-constructed notions of black natural inferiority and the nonunification of the races, explicitly places black women on a lower plane than animals. Lyle claims that his discouragement from dating black women is rooted in the "entire southern heritage" that he "proudly embrace[s]." Throughout his questionnaire, Lyle expresses that white men dating and marrying black women is completely implausible and not even worthy of consideration.

Although the majority of respondents engaged explicit and implicit gendered racism, the explicitly vulgar discourse shared by Lyle and Randy, particularly the comparison of black women to animals, represents only 5.5 percent of respondents. However, addressing such responses is essential, as many in mainstream contemporary society believe that such beliefs have disappeared. Explicit beliefs in the biological difference and inferiority of blacks continue to exist in society today, but capturing this discourse in contemporary research is rather difficult, because it is usually reserved for backstage settings with friends and family members.[8] The online design of this questionnaire provides a virtual backstage for white men and allows for more candid responses.

Strength and Dominance: Black Women as Complicit in Their Own Rejection

In the narrative stories white male respondents tell about black women, they often apply a bevy of characteristics and attributes, such as strength and domination. These attributes were frequently used by respondents to blame black women for their rejection and to define them as justifiably unwanted. These respondents often had very few, if any, personal experiences with black women.

White men in this study who had long-term relationships with black women and who were most attracted to black women were more likely to apply positive attributes to black women or to apply the same attributes, such as strength and independence, yet view these traits as a positive. Only a small proportion of respondents, however, had meaningful relationships and experiences with black women. Only 14 percent of the research sample had long-term relationships, and only 11 percent were most attracted to black women.

Isaac, an upper-middle-class male in his twenties from Pennsylvania, is one of the few white males who dated black women in long-term relationships. Expressing an appreciation of black women, he states what he believes are the attributes of black women: "I think they are more candid and realistic, in addition to hard working/diligent. They understand that the odds are stacked against them yet they still maintain and [have a] good attitude, contrary to popular stereotype." He goes on to list what he finds attractive about black women, including such traits as "candor, affectionate, humorous, outgoing, motivated, great work ethic, intelligent, savvy, friendly, slightly conservative." Likewise, another respondent, Hamilton, a middle-aged Californian, appreciates what he perceives as black women's strength:

> I hate to project any conclusions or generalizations about traits that are race specific based on my own experiences. However, most of the black women I know have a great inner strength and confidence. There is a streak of fighter within them, however, that is probably representative of the black experience in this country.

Hamilton reveals that he has had many personal interactions with black women, including several close black female friends, and he has dated three black women. According to Hamilton, the strength of black women is a positive attribute necessary for dealing with racialized experiences in society.

While a small proportion of respondents viewed black women's strength as a positive, the majority viewed strength and a multitude of other perceived attributes as disadvantageous to relationships. These respondents define black women as strong, domineering, aggressive, attitudinal, bossy, and bitchy and assert that it is, in fact, black women's own fault, because of these personal attributes, that they are unwanted by white men (and men in general).

Russ, a white male from Missouri in his forties with a professional degree, expresses the view of the domineering black woman. He states that a prevalent trait of black women is "the domination of the opposite gender." When asked why the intermarriage rate is low between black women and white men, he extends this perception, stating, "We are stronger than the black man on moral fiber. We will not allow any women to run our life." This respondent states that he has had few personal interactions with black women and no close black female friends, yet he provides a specific narrative of domineering, emasculating black women. Max, a working-class respondent in his thirties who resides in Indiana, shares a similar sentiment:

> You mostly see white women with black men—I don't know why it is not more the other way—I just assume it is because a black woman wouldn't likely put up with a man they can't take care of. An independent man may scare her. Most black men expect that a black woman will take care of them—I think some black women don't know how to take a man who can work and contribute.

Max later states, when asked what would need to change for more white men to marry black women, "Black women need to be more 50–50, they can't control everything. They should want a partner, not a puppet. They should want a man that wants to be a part of the family." Max has had few personal experiences with black women outside of work, and growing up, his family rarely interacted with black families. He has, however, mostly lived in neighborhoods where more than half of the families are black, and he states he "recently had [his] first sexual experience with a black woman." Max and Russ both invoke a central constructed narrative of black women: the emasculating black matriarch. Consider sociologist Daniel Moynihan's 1965 report *The Negro Family: The Case for National Action*; in this report, he provides one of the earliest narratives on the negative black matriarch. He states a "fundamental fact of Negro Americans' family life is the often reversed roles of husband and wife."[9] The matriarchal family for Moynihan was a symbol of the "tangle of pathology" tantamount with black communities.[10] In expressing this long-standing construction of the black matriarch, Max implies that because black women have not accepted the proper edicts of traditional femininity and are domineering matriarchs, white men are not interested.

Norman, a college-educated white male in his twenties from Tennessee, also asserts that black women lack femininity, which he believes is a flaw that affects their ability to form good relationships. The following is his response to what he finds attractive about white women:

> White females are too large a group to generalize in the US. By contrast: Asian girls tend to either follow the stereotype of introverted studiousness or fight it with a very particular kind of sorority culture. There are exceptions, but these are two common personalities and though neither is strongly off-putting to me, neither is very attractive, either. Black girls tend (again, with exceptions) to respond to their competing pressures of being independent and not "being white/bourgeoisie" with an individual-centric position of strength, almost aloofness. I do find this somewhat unattractive as it can lead to selfishness, or at least a lack of openness, in a relationship.

Norman was asked to respond to what he finds attractive about white women, because he stated in response to an earlier question that he is most attracted to white women out of all racial groups of women. He finds this request too difficult to comply with, yet he finds it rather easy to explain in broad strokes the traits he believes characterize Asian American and black women. Norman reveals that he has had only professionally related interactions and "friend of friend" contact with black women. Yet, despite minimal personal interactions, Norman defines black women one-dimensionally as strong, independent, and resistant to traditional femininity. When asked if he can find his ideal woman among black women, he states,

> No, I do not ... black girls face pressures that white girls do not and respond to those pressures. One of the pressures that they are under is to be "authentic". Black high school kids who make straight A's will have 1.5 fewer friends of the same race as white kids who make the same grades.

> There is a force in the black community that resists academic achievement; it is seen as selling out.... The push for "authenticity" reaches beyond grades and, combined with a lack of reliable black men in committed, long-term relationships to serve as role models, it results in many black girls being opposed to a soft femininity because it is "weak." They don't want to be vulnerable.

Norman provides several commonly held white constructed assertions and assumptions about blacks and the value of education. In addition, he believes black women's depraved culture leads them to adapt traits and attributes that are unfeminine. However, in a society in which black women face challenging experiences, in which they must spend psychic energy resisting the negative construction of their bodies, their continued struggle with racism, sexism, and classism, being "weak" or "vulnerable" (soft femininity) has never been much of an option for many black women.

Jeff, an upper-middle-class white male in his thirties from Tennessee, also expresses a view of black women's inordinate strength. He, too, views this strength as a detriment to the type of relationships black women can form. Jeff has had very few personal interactions with black women outside of work-related experiences and shares a similar, yet slightly different, perspective with Norman:

> Not trying to be racist, but so many black women are angry, many times for good reason as the lack of responsibility shown by many black males leaves many women of color with a burden, but black women seem to take so much pride in being a "strong black woman" that it comes at the price of relations with other people. I have had too many black male friends to count, by only have 1 women I can claim.

Jeff is correct in that black women's intraracial relationships have faced peril, including the high mortality and incarceration rates of black men and the effects of black men's interracial marriage rates,[11] resulting in a higher likelihood of black women who are single, never married, and/or single mothers. However, Jeff gives black women a limited license to be angry about various relationship experiences with black men. It is important to note that strength is often a survival strategy black women employ to manage experiences they have encountered in the relationship sphere. Black women have been constructed as a body of strength by whites since before the fifteenth century,[12] but this was to benefit a slave economy that thrived on black female childbirth and free labor. With the perils of slavery and legal segregation, being strong was often the only option afforded black women, and black women have had to be strong in order to survive, cope, and resist, whether within the broader white society or within their own black communities. And although indelibly embracing strength and long suffering has detrimental effects on black women's health and peace of mind,[13] it has been a more than adequate survival method and one that many black women are unapologetically proud of.

Jeff not only blamed black women's strength for their undesirability but, more specifically, he blamed black women for stepping outside the bounds of "femininity" and using strength for survival. Jeff holds to a long-standing patriarchal perspective that women, to be available and attractive to men, must not be too strong or too independent; otherwise, men will be unneeded. From a Foucauldian perspective,[14] women are expected to discipline their bodies, in terms of physical looks, personality, and traits, to "conform" to "patriarchal norms of femininity."[15] Thus, black women, even in the face of peril, must grin and bear it, must always maintain a degree of femininity, and must never be so angry that they engage in survival strategies that hover on masculine identities. While Jeff admonishes black women for not adhering to feminine norms and places them as the source of their own rejection, he makes it clear that he is capable of forming lasting relationships with black men, assumedly because of a bond rooted in shared patriarchal notions of masculinity. Jeff's discourse suggests that the reason for black women's rejection is black women; if only they embraced traditional feminine norms, then they, too, could be loveable, but because they do not, they are an undesirable female body.

Not Even Wanted by Black Men

Black men interracially marry at more than twice the rate of black women; 357,000 of the total 504,000 black-white non-Hispanic marriages in 2010 consisted of black men and white women.[16] Several respondents note the greater prevalence of black men–white women interracial relationships, and some of these respondents provide their assessment as to why the difference exists. Martin, an upper-middle-class male from Iowa, states the following:

> It is higher between black men and white women because 1—status symbol 2—dominance thing (see a lot of black men sodomizing white blondes than white men doing the nasty with black women—just go to any porn site to prove this) 3—more acceptable to be black male, white female 4—present fad.

In his statement, Martin defines white women as the "status symbol," essentially the pinnacle of true womanhood and beauty in society that black men must have. The implication here is that while white women are a prize to have on one's arm, black women certainly are not. Bern, a college-educated male in his forties from Virginia, responds similarly when asked why he thinks the intermarriage rate is low between black women and white men:

> I think that black men date and marry white women because they are considered a trophy for them. It is telling white men that they can get their women. 100 years ago, if a white woman was seen with a black man, she would be beaten and him shot. For white women, it is forbidden, taboo love. It wasn't thought much of if a white man had a black woman, it was just for sex.

Black women have long been constructed as the anti-woman,[17] and hence the anti–trophy wife (unless they are similar to white women in looks). Influential sexologist Havelock Ellis, in his 1927 work *Studies in the Psychology of Sex*, intimates that there is an objective, not constructed, standard of beauty, one that is "fundamentally" the same throughout the world. According to Ellis, this "objective" beauty is found "commonly" and in "perfection among the white peoples of Europe."[18] He states that "savages" or "lower races" admire European "beauty" and find the people of their own race that are "half-caste" (members "crossed with white persons") more attractive than "their own women of pure race."[19] Whites, because of their power in the world, have been successful in globally defining European beauty as the fundamental standard. However, this beauty standard is not an objective fact, but a social construction by those in power. The construction of the European beauty standard is deeply embedded in the deep frames of many whites and some people of color and is viewed unquestioningly as commonsense.

Bern, whose personal interactions with black women are only work related, states the following when asked if he would ever form a relationship with a black woman: "Maybe I am prejudice. I would be afraid [of] what friends or family would think about me dating a black woman." He goes on to state that he would only date black women under "total secrecy," and that he is most interested in a sexual relationship. Asked under what condition(s), if any, would he marry a black woman he responded, "She would have to have a lot of money." For Bern, black women are still only good for closeted sexual relationships shrouded in secrecy; they are women he should be ashamed of wanting or being seen with in public, white settings.

Taking a different perspective, Jeff, a respondent mentioned in a prior section of this chapter, reveals that he believes that black men and white women's interracial relationships are rooted in the sexual stereotype of black men:

> I think that while i[t] has been more common to see acceptance of black male white female relationships, and it is well known that 3 times as many white women have sex with black men discreetly, the same is not true in black women. [W]hite women mainly are interested in large penises of black men. [B]ut for white men black women simply don't bring enough to the table (Asian women are petite and supposedly more submissive), (Latino women are insatiable and have curvaceous bodies).

From Jeff's viewpoint, white women's interest in black men is supposedly rooted in black men's "physical endowments" and "sexual prowess" (a strong stereotype central to how black male bodies have been constructed), whereas black women, in his view, possess no special or exotic stereotype to entice white men as Latina and Asian American women do.

Some respondents tacitly define black women as a generally mistreated and unappreciated group, particularly by the men in their own racial group. Respondents, in a surprising finding, go so far as to claim that black women are not even desirable to black men, providing an overall narrative of black women as universally unwanted bodies.

Lyle (mentioned earlier), who engages in strong racist and sexist language, reveals that he believes black men do

Narratives of the Unwanted Woman 99

not prefer black women. When asked what would discourage him from dating black women, he states, "Well, society would frown upon it plus why would I date a negro when there is a plethora of pretty white women? Even negro males prefer to date white women ... go figure."

Similarly, Tyler, an upper-middle-class male in his twenties who resides in Kansas, juxtaposes black women's status with white women's. He states, "They seem like they are below us. Where black men see white women as a trophy, white men see black women as the opposite. Not even good enough for a black man." Tyler intimates that white men get their cue from black men, whom whites constructed as the bottom of the racial hierarchy. Thus if black men do not want black women, why would white men?

Tyler, who has had few personal interactions with black women, continues his negative description of black women when asked if he could find his ideal woman among black women, "[N]o, because many black women are loud and lack the humbleness required of a [C]hristian wife." Here again, black women are described as disregarding proper feminine edicts (as well as the continued regard for a certain type of femininity) making them undesirable relationship partners.

Roger, mentioned earlier, unabashedly expresses the following about black women: "To me, it seems the average black woman is a ghetto, loud mouthed, obnoxious, bitchy, and hateful." He later states that this "would be enough to turn any man away."

Similarly, Skip, a middle-aged, lower-middle-class respondent from Alabama, shares the following when responding to why he thinks the intermarriage rate is low between black women and white men: "Because so damn many black women are just domineering and bitchy as hell." "Bitch," in a racialized patriarchal society is a way to "stigmatize" black women who do not demonstrate middle-class ideals of "passivity" and "submissiveness."[20] Skip's and Roger's descriptions of the domineering "black bitch" place black women outside the bounds of white-constructed traditional femininity and blame them for their own rejection. Responding to what he believed would need to change for more white men to marry black women, Skip contends,

> The domineering, neck wagging attitudes also would have to pretty much disappear. No man wants that, not even black men. Marriage in the black community between black women and black men is also (comparatively) drastically low. This [is] because black men don't like that neck wagging anymore than white men.

Skip describes himself as having had five or more black girlfriends, and these relationships were mainly sexual. And, for a period of time, he was a sex addict and predominantly "sought out" black female prostitutes. Outside of sexual relationships, he describes his main experiences with black women as acquaintanceships in his current church. Despite his negative views of black women as domineering bitches and the sole cause of spoiled interracial/intraracial relationships, Skip regularly sought out black women for short-term sexual relationships and encounters. This contradictory behavior is a common one and reveals the complexity in white men's perceptions of black women.

The Complexity of White Men's Views: Grappling with Sexual Desire

White men's perceptions of black women are often conflicting, as they grapple with both strong views of them as anti-women and strong sexual desires for them. Rooted in the white construction of black female bodies as the embodiment of innate heightened "animalistic" sexuality, white men have sexually desired black bodies for a long time. While black female sexuality is viewed as "disruptive to the prevailing social and moral order," it is also exoticized and fantasized about by white men.[21] According to bell hooks, these fantasies are an intense desire to "get a bit of the other." As the sexual body of the "other" invokes both danger and resignation, it is also constructed as possessing "more exciting" and "more intense" pleasure.[22] Through black female bodies, white men can seek and release those peculiar, uninhibited desires.

Several respondents express generally derogatory views of black women despite simultaneously projecting exoticized sexuality on them in the form of sexual fantasies, attraction, and desires. Tyler, mentioned in an earlier section of this chapter, views black women as "not even good enough for a black man." Later in his questionnaire, when asked whether or not he would be intimidated by black women, he explicitly declared, "[N]o, I feel like I am better than them." Although Tyler does not view any black women as a desirable wife or as his ideal woman, he admits to having two sexual relationships with black women and says that his interest in black women is of a purely sexual nature. According to Tyler, "darker skin and sexual appetites" was the source of his interest in the two black women with whom he engaged in sexual relationships. Despite Tyler's view that black women are not on the same level as him, or black men, he sought sex with them.

Consider also Vernon, a college-educated respondent from New York. According to Vernon, black women are predominantly "[l]oud and verbally abusive. Violent and I have been near some that had an unpleasant odor." Vernon, like other respondents, describes black women as violent and abusive, characteristics more commonly used to describe black men. He applies these very negative traits to black women, despite admittedly having almost no contact with blacks, as he states that he has mostly lived in neighborhoods with no black families, has no black female friends, has never dated a black woman, and has had virtually no personal interactions with black women, aside from having sex with a black prostitute. He goes on to deem it necessary for black women to have a strong racial identity, because "they are not on the whole desired among other groups." Although he describes most black women as "unattractive," he states that he wishes black women were more open to interracial relationships. However, his interest in interracial relationships is purely sexual. He is interested in fulfilling his uninhibited sexual desires with a black female body, as he sought in the past with the black prostitute. Furthermore, he shared a particular sexual fantasy he has of a black woman:

> I like the thought of having a black woman with bigger lips for oral sex. I like the thought of having anal sex with a black woman with a big round butt but she should not be too heavy. I would like [to] give oral sex to a black woman with clear not too blotchy skin.

In this sexualized fantasy, black women's body parts, their lips and buttocks, are separated from their whole selves and nothing more than exotic sexual parts commoditized for white male desire.

Max, mentioned earlier, also engages in discourse that presents black women as sexual objects. Max does not express the explicit notions of black women as violent and abusive like Vernon, but he does express strong views of black women as domineering matriarchs. Additionally, while Max reveals that he is open to forming romantic relationships with black women, he is not open to marrying black women, citing interracial children as the deterrent. Like other respondents, he states that he has had rare personal interactions with black women outside of work and his only non-work-related interaction is his recent "first sexual experience with a black woman." He goes on to state that what he finds sexually attractive about black women are their "big lips and soft round bodies." In a subsequent comment, when asked to share his opinions about black women, he stated, "[T]he darker the meat the sweeter the treat."

Max describes black women as a sexual experiment, like an exotic car he took for a joy ride for the first time. This experiment of seeking sex with the dark other is a way, according to bell hooks, that whites can "leave behind white 'innocence' and enter the world of 'experience,'" as it is assumed that naturally the dark other is more experienced in the realm of the sensual.[23] An experience with the dark other represents a sort of sexual "rite of passage"; this is especially true from a historical perspective, as young white men, sons of slave owners and later sons of legal segregationists, sought black female bodies for sexual experience.[24] Max's expressed desire for the "big lips" of black women again characterizes black women's body parts as an exotic commodity for intensified sexual pleasure. His projection of "dark meat" as some sort of intensified sexual indulgence is rooted in the construction of the body of the other as alive, primitive, dangerous, and an exotic pleasure that cannot be found in whites. Another respondent, Brent, an upper-middle-class Mississippian in his forties, describes the thrill of "taboo" sex with black women:

> I guess some of the attraction is the Taboo feelings of black and white mixing but I also enjoy the passion; the contrast of black on white sex and the fantasy of being the first white man a black woman might have.

Brent does not apply explicitly negative characteristics to black women as did other respondents discussed in this section; nevertheless, he reveals that he views black women as a sexual thrill intensified by the "taboo" nature of the sexual mixing. He has dated three black women but states that these relationships were mainly sexual and the type of relationship he would most likely seek with a black woman is a sexual one.

The white male respondents discussed in this section, while predominantly holding strongly derogatory views of black women, simultaneously sexually fantasize, desire, and project sexual powers onto black female bodies. Their penchant for "big lips," their desire for "big butts" for intensified anal sex, and their want for "darker skin" as indication of a strong "sexual appetite" are a reification of gendered and raced myths that maintain white domination[25] and control over black female sexual body parts in a commodity culture. These white men's deep frames negligently allow them to think of this as simply sexual desire and openness to experiencing the "black other,"[26] and not as the perpetuation of gendered racism that it is.

Chapter Summary

Racialized and gendered narratives are central components embedded in the deep frames of the white dominant group (and other racial groups), buttressing their privileged position, while confirming the subordinate place of people of color in society. Describing black women as too strong, domineering, bitchy, animalistic, and diseased, white male respondents perpetuate old narratives that tell the story of the unwanted black woman. These stories label black women as unwanted not only by white men but even by men of their own racial group. These narratives declare the attributes and behaviors of black women as explanation of their undesirability and implicate them in their own rejection. While respondents often defined black women as an undesirable and rejected body, many harbored sexual fantasies and sought sexual encounters with black women. The licentious black jezebel, who has animalistic sexual powers, is a central white-constructed narrative of black women. Historically, this narrative justified white men's rape of black women, and contemporarily, it justifies the desire for sex-only encounters with black women, while not affecting white men's reputations in the white community. Respondents ascribed a bevy of negative attributes to black women, despite most having few, if any, personal interactions with them. Guided by centuries-old, white-constructed, racialized, and gendered narratives in their deep frames, personal experiences are unnecessary and contemporary white men are disciplined to view black women as undesirable, illegitimate relationship partners.

Notes

1. Richard Delgado, "Storytelling for Oppositionists and Others: A Plea for Narrative," in *Critical Race Theory: The Cutting Edge*, 2nd ed., ed. Richard Delgado and Jean Stefancic (Philadelphia: Temple University Press, 2000), p. 60.
2. bell hooks, *Ain't I a Woman: Black Women and Feminism* (Boston: South End Press, 1981).
3. Patricia H. Collins, *Black Sexual Politics: African Americans, Gender, and the New Racism* (New York: Routledge, 2005).
4. Kimberle Crenshaw, "Race, Reform, and Retrenchment: Transformation and Legitimation in Antidiscrimination Law," in *Critical Race Theory*, ed. Kimberle Crenshaw, Neal Gotanda, Gary Peller, and Kendall Thomas (New York: The New Press, 1995), p. 113.
5. Thomas Jefferson, *Notes on the State of Virginia*, ed. David Waldstreicher (New York: Penguin Classics, [1785] 2002), p. 177.
6. Sander L. Gilman, *Difference and Pathology: Stereotypes of Sexuality, Race, and Madness* (Ithaca, NY: Cornell University Press, 1985).
7. Evelyn M. Hammonds, "Toward a Genealogy of Black Female Sexuality: The Problematic of Silence," in *Feminist Genealogies, Colonial Legacies, Democratic Futures*, ed. Jacqui Alexander and Chandra Mohanty (New York: Routledge, 1997), p.170–182.
8. Leslie H. Picca and Joe R. Feagin, *Two-Faced Racism: Whites in the Backstage and Frontstage* (New York: Routledge, 2007).
9. Daniel Moynihan, *The Negro Family: The Case for National Action* (Washington, DC: U.S. Government Printing Office, 1965), p. 30.

10. Ibid.

11. Kyle D. Crowder and Stewart E. Tolnay, "A New Marriage Squeeze for Black Women: The Role of Racial Intermarriage by Black Men," *Journal of Marriage and the Family* 62 (2000): 792–807.

12. Jennifer L. Morgan, "'Some Could Suckle over Their Shoulder': Male Travelers, Female Bodies, and the Gendering of Racial Ideology, 1500–1770," in *Skin Deep, Spirit Strong: The Black Female Body in American Culture*, ed. Kimberly Wallace-Sanders (Ann Arbor: University of Michigan Press, 2002), pp. 37–65.

13. Charisse Jones and Kumea Shorter-Gooden, *Shifting: The Double Lives of Black Women in America* (New York: HarperCollins, 2003).

14. Michel Foucault, *Discipline and Punish: The Birth of the Prison* (New York: Vintage Books, 1977).

15. Tina Chanter, *Gender: Key Concepts in Philosophy* (New York: Continuum, 2006), p. 60.

16. U.S. Bureau of the Census, *Interracial Married Couples: 1980 to 2002* (Washington, DC: U.S. Government Printing Office, 2004).

17. See hooks, *Ain't I a Woman*.

18. Havelock Ellis, *Studies in the Psychology of Sex, Volume IV: Sexual Selection in Man: I. Taste, II. Smell, III. Hearing, IV. Vision* (Philadelphia, PA: Davis Co., 1927), p. 40.

19. Ibid.

20. Collins, *Black Sexual Politics*, p. 138.

21. Stephen N. Haymes, "White Culture and the Politics of Racial Difference," in *Multicultural Education, Critical Pedagogy and the Politics of Difference*, ed. C. E. Sleeter and P. L. McLaren (Albany: State University of New York Press, 1995), p. 117.

22. bell hooks, *Black Looks: Race and Representation* (Boston: South End Press, 1992), p. 23.

23. Ibid.
24. Ibid.
25. Ibid.
26. Ibid.

Chapter V

Conclusion
The Disciplinary Power of the Deep Frame

Power in contemporary society habitually passes itself off as embodied in the normal as opposed to the superior. This is common to all forms of power, but it works in a peculiarly seductive way with whiteness, because of the way it seems rooted, in commonsense thought, in things other than ethnic difference.[1]

Deep Frame, Power, and Discipline

Power in modern society is not just the process of a top-down ruling effect but, according to Foucault, is also "bottom-to-top and laterally."[2] Power is not simply a ruling elite wielding power from above, but a disciplinary power that is "absolutely indiscreet since it is everywhere and always alert" and "absolutely discreet for it functions permanently and largely in silence."[3] Inherent in this disciplinary power of society are whiteness, patriarchy, and elitism, which are often hard to recognize or analyze because they are so embodied in the normal. White elites have created and legitimized knowledge and meaning systems in society historically and presently, and this is the knowledge/information in the deep frames of contemporary whites (and many people of color in society). Deep frames, the infrastructure of the mind, operate in an automatic and unconscious manner, and appear commonsensical.

Whites in overtly powerful positions and average, everyday whites who may feel they have no or very little power in society, through the social action of discourse, are able to discursively pass on their deep framing. Thus, the construction of whites as virtuous, beautiful, hardworking, and the ideal entity, as well as the construction of blacks as unattractive, lazy, and promiscuous, is continuously learned. Whites are able to pass on important components of their deep framing of black women, including emotions and racialized, gendered, and classed discourse, often through segregated family and friend interactions (backstage settings). In this research sample, over 50 percent of the white male respondents state that they had been either discouraged from dating black women, explicitly and implicitly, by family and friends, and at times by black men, or told negative things about black people at some point in their lives by family members and friends. Those in power, most often white male elites, also have the most access to the media[4] and thus the ability to create, control, and influence public media images as well as to control and/or influence the language and discourse used in mainstream newspapers, news shows, and politics.

Consider Tyler, a respondent mentioned in earlier chapters. He comments on the effect of the media, stating, "[T]he women we see on [C]omedy [C]entral and in *[B]arbershop* are how we view all women of black color." Important here is not so much that there are images that may fit a particular stereotype specific to the construction of black women, which is problematic, but the fact that there is not a multiplicity of media images showing diverse representations of black women. This shortfall is further compounded because a multiplicity of images and portrayals of black women in the media does not mean the media will counteract a white male's deep frame, as simply refuting the frame can oftentimes reinforce it.[5] Moreover, if more positive media portrayals of black women are to counteract the deep frames of respondents such as Tyler, such positive images must have a frame to hang on to.[6]

The 14 percent of white male respondents who had more meaningful experiences with black women (long-term relationships) can better understand the dynamics of the media, which often acts in ways to reinforce white men's deep frames, and are better able to resist them. Consider Brice, a lower-middle-class New Yorker in his twenties who reveals that he has close black female friends and has dated a black woman in a long-term relationship. Critically, he states,

> I feel that media, entertainment, and an individual's environment provides us with our judgment on black females. Having the ability to socialize with females of the opposite sex and see beyond the stereotypes have brought me to respect and acknowledge the beauty and intelligence of black females.

In this statement, Brice recognizes that he views limited images of black women in the media as well as acknowledges the role of the environment, which can include family and friends, on his perspectives of black women. However, because he has had valuable and long-term experiences with black women, he is able to resist the racialized and gendered construction of black women that is so pervasive in society. Brice's comments show a level of complexity: People are not just agency-less bodies; they can engage in resistance against many components of their deep framing. However, that resistance is often predicated on the type of counter-experiences they have had. Resisting the racialized and gendered information in one's deep frame is difficult, particularly for whites but also for some people of color, because this information is pervasive throughout all aspects of society and is normalized as common sense, fact, and reality. Whites may not recognize, although some certainly do, that their deep frames consist of a constructed knowledge system privileging whites in power and maintaining hierarchical race, gender, and class dynamics. Black cultural inferiority (and even biological inferiority) and white colorblindness are important segments of information in the deep frames of contemporary white men and are integral in upholding oppression. Whites can state that they are not bigots (as many respondents do in this research), while claiming cultural inferiority as explanation of black women's "undesirability." The hegemonic discourses of their deep frames treat as fact and as normal—not as racialized, gendered, or classed—the notion of black women's inferiority as women and as relationship partners. Hence, resisting one's framing proves difficult, because the knowledge within it is often perceived as fact, or even opinion, but not as perpetuating racism, sexism, and classism.

Also important is that many white men can effectively view black women as unfeminine and undesirable women, and some can view them as inhuman, all while having no or very little contact with black women. Consider the fact that some of the strongest vulgar and negative thoughts about black women came predominantly from those white men with the least amount of experiences and legitimate personal interactions with black women. Thus, most everything these respondents felt, thought, and perceived about black women came from their deep frames. As noted earlier, white men's thoughts, opinions, and perspectives of black women are often not considered, by whites, as perpetuating racist, sexist, or classist ideals. They are often simply viewed as opinions and thoughts unaffected by outside forces but based on truth and sheer individualization. However, the racialized, gendered, and classed views held by white men are not "personal opinion about other groups, but a shared group-based attitude towards another (mostly dominated) group, and hence [are] often associated with relations of group dominance and power."[7] The thoughts and opinions expressed discursively by the white male respondents are reflections of existing power structures that aid in the legitimization and maintenance of the power and status of whites in society.

White men's deep frames not only shape how they view, perceive, and emote regarding black women, but most significantly, they shape the types of interactions white men will seek with black women, essentially disciplining their behavior where black women are concerned and the types of relationships that will form. James, a respondent mentioned in earlier chapters, shows the disciplinary power of his deep frame in the following quote:

> I have never thought of black women as potential romantic partners, more friends, co-workers, matronly types. Most of the black women I have known were married. I am not racist but I grew up in such a racist environment that I cannot completely shake the notion that black women are out of bounds for a white man.

James admits to growing up in a racist environment, yet he does not consider himself racist, despite the fact that he engages strong discriminatory discourse earlier in his questionnaire when he describes black culture as "inferior" to white and defines only black women with "less prominent" black features as attractive. For James, this appears to be a simple representation of fact. Hence, he has not only been disciplined by his deep frame to view too black women as, at best, less attractive, he has also been disciplined to view them as friends, workers, and "matronly" types, a combination representing a modern-day reassuring and comforting black mammy. He has been disciplined to understand that black women are outside of the stipulations of femininity, beauty, and proper culture, and thus he views them as "out of bounds" as a legitimate relationship partner.

The disciplinary power of white men's deep frames varies. For many white men, their deep frames discipline them from forming any type of relationship with black women (outside of friendship or work-related interactions), as with James. However, some white men may be disciplined to form relationships, yet never seek marriage with black women. These white men may seek dating in an open relationship known to all, while others are disciplined to keep those relationships private and hidden from close family members and friends, as is the case with Bern, who states that he would only date a black woman under "total secrecy." Still others may solely seek sexual relationships with black women, rooted in the projection of licentious sexuality on black female bodies, as is shown by several respondents in this study, yet they are disciplined to not consider black women as desirable "legitimate" partners outside of the sexual act. There are also white men who may actively seek real relationships with black women that are not predicated on sexual eroticization. These white men may be more likely to have a deep frame with more critical knowledge about race and gender dynamics in society. Yet, only 6 of 134 respondents revealed a general understanding of how racist and sexist systems impact the life experiences of black women and affect how white men view black women. Hence, the material reality of the low intermarriage rate of black women and white men, the overall exclusion of black women by white men as dating partners, and the small percentage of white men who have had long-term relationships with black women, as found in my research sample, illustrates that many white men have deep frames with hegemonic information about black women and it is difficult to resist against the disciplinary power of their deep framing.

The Implications

Impact on Other Relationships

In bell hooks's critical work *Black Looks: Race and Representation*, she provides a critical analysis of the 1930s film *Imitation of Life* and the 1980s film *Choose Me*. Both of these films portray highly sexualized multiracial black women chasing after a white man who does not want them and who easily discards them. The message that both the older and the more contemporary films convey according to hooks is the black woman who "chase[s] the white man as if only he had the power to affirm that she is truly desirable."[8] This is an important point that hooks makes, and one that I would like to stress here. The purpose of engaging this research was not to seek white male validation or imply that black women must have white male validation to be beautiful and desirable. This research analyzes white men because their position in society, as both white and male, allows them to control and influence hegemonic ideas in society. Elite white men have played a central role in the construction of knowledge and meaning systems in U.S. and global society. Historically, influential European males were the catalyst behind the construction of black women as deviant and pathological. By means of friends, family, media, politics, and other important structures of society, contemporary white men continually regenerate and pass on the construction of black women as the opposite of hegemonic (white) femininity and as undesirable bodies.

This construction of black women is continuously embedded in the deep frames of not only white men but also men of color, including black men, thus ultimately affecting both interracial and intraracial heterosexual relationships for black women. As discussed in Chapter I, black women do not have a significant interracial marriage rate with any men of color. In contrast, white women have more significant intermarriage with black, Latino, and multiracial men.[9] The deep frames of Asian Americans, Latinos, and Native Americans (as well as black men) are susceptible to and affected by the disciplinary power of white men's construction of black women, and thus these groups may also view black women as undesirable. A study by Neiman, Rozelle, Baxter, and Sullivan found that Hispanics held predominantly negative stereotypes of black women as "egotistical," "unmannerly," "antagonistic," "lower-class," "ambitionless," and as having "dark skin."[10] Hence, Latinos and other racial groups of color also have deep frames of negative information about black women, which affects the types of relationships and interactions they seek with black women, particularly for those racial groups with hopes of moving up the racial hierarchy through seeking acceptance among white communities.

The deep frames of black men and women also include racialized, gendered, and classed information about black women, constructed by elite historic white men, which influences how black men and women view black women's worthiness as relationship partners. Hence, black women with darker skin and more black facial features and hair textures are not just deemed less attractive by white men, but also by some black men and women. A 2002 study by Mark E. Hill examines how black men and women, growing up in different periods, including a cohort of individuals coming of age during the black power and "black is beautiful" movements, rank the attractiveness of black women (and men) who range in skin color. Overwhelmingly, the study shows that black male and female perceivers ranked the black women with the lightest skin color as the most attractive on a seven-point attractiveness scale, whereas only four black women with the darkest skin were given a high attractiveness rating. Hill states that these findings are not statistically different across sex, age, education, or region, and thus black men and women had similar views about black women, skin color, and attractiveness. Additionally, those blacks coming of age during the "black is beautiful" movement were just as likely to have "color biases" as those not coming of age during that period of black empowerment.[11]

A mainstream example is the public judgment of the wives of National Basketball Association (NBA) players. I reviewed a website showing both black and white/European NBA players' wives and girlfriends where people (I could not decipher their races) could leave comments. White wives, of black and white basketball players, who were attractive but did not fit the supermodel stereotype were considered attractive or no comment was made. Black wives of basketball players who had a fair or light brown complexion and straight or naturally wavy hair were viewed as pretty and worthy of being married to a professional basketball player. However, black NBA players with attractive wives who had darker skin, a medium-size build, and hair styles without weaves, wigs, or naturally straight or wavy hair were often viewed as unattractive; some were even ridiculed by those who left comments. The majority of the Internet comments defined those black women who were attractive, yet did not represent a European phenotype, as not beautiful enough for the black male athlete they married. Conversely, the commenters defined those white women who were attractive, but not of supermodel status, satisfactory partners for the black or white male athletes they married. For example, a commenter (on a different website) stated the following about a popular NBA player's wife, who is an attractive woman with a dark brown complexion and neck-length straight hair:

> Have you seen [NBA player's name] wife ... ugh! She looks like a burnt piece of chicken! Damn, I'd rather give up my 17 percent in child support than to have her on my arm during

interview time. I know [NBA player's name] is a real grounded person but damn he needs to throw her (creature from the black lagoon ass) back in the Mississippi mudwater. She is definitely not your typical glamorous NBA wife.[12]

This commenter's statement makes a vicious reference to the woman's dark brown skin tone, equating her skin color not only with unattractiveness but as outside the bounds of humanity, as he compares her to a fictitious monster from a 1950s horror film.

The marital union of Usher Raymond, a famous rhythm and blues singer, with Tameka Foster (they have since divorced) represents yet another prominent example. Fans, Internet bloggers, and tabloids voiced much ambivalence toward this relationship (particularly when it initially developed). Some of the arguments coming from black men and women (from which *Essence* notes some of the harshest criticism came) against the relationship included Foster's seven-year age advantage over Raymond and her status as a divorced single mother of two. Others claimed that Foster was a gold digger and only with Raymond because of his wealth, despite the fact that she has been a successful celebrity stylist for ten years.[13] Most significantly, many of the arguments against Raymond and Foster's relationship define Foster, who has a dark-brown-skinned complexion and does not appear to have naturally wavy, curly, or straight hair, as unattractive and not pretty enough for Usher Raymond. In a 2007 interview, Foster commented on the grasp the nonblack standard of beauty has on blacks: "We don't like ourselves. If I were Hispanic, Usher would have the sexiest wife alive. If I were mixed, he'd have the sexiest wife alive. But he has a black girl, and it's like, she's horrible and she's ugly. Okay maybe I don't fit the cookie cutter standard—twenty-five and a size two. But this is who he loves."[14]

These examples of black intraracial relationships reveal how the deep frames of black men and women include a white construction of black women as less beautiful than the European standard, which disciplines how even blacks view the beauty of black women. Even as some black women and men resist, many blacks continue to judge their own beauty against the normative white standard, which in turn disciplines black men and black women on the type of intraracial partners they seek. Moreover, the example of how black and white NBA players' wives were viewed by online commenters shows the entrenchment of racialized notions of beauty. Many may see black women as experiencing beauty standards no different from white women. However, this is a false assumption, because white women *are* the standard of beauty, and black women will "never become white."[15]

Black Women's Resistance and Coping Strategies

Consequently, black women have developed methods of resisting the negative ways they have been constructed by white men. Historically and contemporarily, black women resist the way they are viewed, perceived, and interpreted in society and have oftentimes attempted to redefine themselves as a source of empowerment.

Historically, black women resisted the negative construction of their bodies as animalistic, sexually deviant, anti-woman, and the opposite of hegemonic white femininity through various means. During slavery, black women did not just passively accept their fate, but many resisted harshly or subtly, all attempting to find ways to fight against oppression. For example, many enslaved women feigned illness, fought back, and endured severe punishment to avoid the sexual abuse of slave masters and overseers.[16] Enslaved women often did not want their children to endure the harsh life of slavery and did not want to perpetuate the system of oppression that they were bound to through the reproduction of new generations of black slave bodies. Thus, enslaved women fought against aiding in the exploitative system of interminable slavery by resisting enforced reproduction through the use of contraceptives, abortives, and even infanticide.[17]

After slavery, black women continued to resist oppression and the overriding societal discourse that presented them as licentious jezebels and antifeminine. Historian Darlene Clark Hines, in her study of Midwestern black women in the early 1900s, found that black women engaged in a "culture of dissemblance." By "dissemblance," Hines means the "behavior and attitudes of Black women that created the appearance of openness and disclosure but actually shielded the truth of their inner lives and selves from their oppressors." In this culture of dissemblance, black women silenced and at times denied their sexuality as a way to fight against the overriding sexual myths of black female bodies and to gain a level of respect from society. A number of black women, realizing their vulnerability to rape and domestic abuse, attempted to make their sexuality invisible with hopes of gaining protection from such assaults.[18]

Many black women in the early 1900s wanted to fulfill traditional gender roles, which decreed that women stay at home as opposed to work. According to hooks, black women resented the exploitative circumstances that "forced them to work." However, most black women, historically, did not have a choice regarding their labor force participation, due to the oppressive circumstances of black women's lives and a post-antebellum society dependent on exploited black labor. However, when possible, middle-class black women stayed home and cared for their children as opposed to working outside the home and attempted to resist pervading notions of them as strong anti-women who did not deserve the "leisure time" and status of womanhood afforded to white women.[19]

Black women in contemporary times, as in the past, have not passively accepted the negative construction of their bodies; instead, they have articulated new spaces of self-definition, despite the pervading hegemonic construction that attempts to keep them boxed, limited, and one-dimensional. A central way that black women resist is through constructing a counter-frame, which according to Feagin includes "cognitive elements ... distinctive language of resistance, that are linked to collective understandings about black and white Americans, and U.S. society in general."[20] In a society that has not accepted black women on their own terms, black women have counter-framed, for example, by defining their own beauty standards for hair through the resurgence of natural hair styles, including twists, locs, braids, kinky-curly styles, and the more elaborate hair designs found in popular black hair shows. Black women have also created several popular natural hair blogs, such as Curly Nikki and Texture Playground—sites that embrace black women's natural hair textures and beauty.

Black women have resisted the sexualization of black female bodies within the black community as well. Some hip hop music and videos are used to promote misogynistic notions of black women as gold diggers, hos, and modern jezebels—presenting black women as a smorgasbord of sexual commodities for male desires. And despite the fact that some black women have used the construction of their bodies as deviant sexuality for economic gain by playing the video ho or vixen, other black women have used hip hop music and videos, among other media, as a way to resist negative imagery and embrace their sexuality on their own terms. Queen Latifah, a quintessential black female rapper of the 1990s, and more recently a successful actress and singer, is an example of a black woman using hip hop and her popular television show of the 1990s, *Living Single*, to resist the construction of black female bodies as sexual commodities to be used and mistreated by men (and women). The words to Latifah's 1990s Grammy-winning song "U.N.I.T.Y." exemplify that source of resistance as she denigrates men for disrespecting black women through the use of the derogatory terms "bitch" and "ho." In this song, Latifah poignantly articulates that black women are deserving of respect, and she calls for black women to stand up for themselves and refuse to accept disrespect, belittling, and commoditization of their bodies.

According to Jones and Shorter-Gooden, black women "shift" to cope and survive in a society that constructs them harmfully. Jones and Shorter-Gooden developed this concept in their *African American Women's Voices Project*, which analyzes black women's experiences of racism and sexism from the narratives of black women. Shifting occurs when "African American women change the way they think of things or the expectations they have for themselves. Or they alter their outer appearance. They modify their speech. They shift in one direction at work ... then another at home.... They adjust the way they act in one context for another."[21] Black women shift in a variety of ways to cope with as well as resist the oppressive way their femininity has been constructed. They learn at a very young age to shift their hair "to manage society's limited tolerance of black hair."[22] Thus, they may change their hairstyles, adopting chemically processed hair, weaves, or wigs deemed more "professional," to ensure "that they aren't immediately dismissed based on their hairdos, and that they're given a chance to demonstrate their competence and skills."[23] Black women also shift in relationships, because black women are constructed as strong and essentially long-suffering. Jones and Shorter-Gooden find that, when dealing with black men, black women may shift out of the way and essentially silence themselves to let black men be in control. Important to note is black women may also resist the construction of their bodies as inadequate heterosexual partners for black men, white men, and men of other racial and ethnic groups by opting out of heterosexual relationships. They may choose other forms of partnerships, or they may opt out of partnerships altogether. Shifting as a form of resistance and coping may be explicit in some examples, or black women may engage more tacit tactics—hence they may shift to either explicitly resist the construction of their bodies or they may silence themselves to surreptitiously avoid bringing attention to the way they have been socially constructed.

Significance of This Research

This research represents one of the few critical studies on white men's perspectives on race and gender dynamics.[24] Using the Internet as a virtual backstage setting, I was able to gather invaluable and candid information on contemporary white men's deep frames, to elucidate white men's consistent exclusion of black women as relationship partners. This research problematizes the findings of current interracial marriage theorists, who, after debunking the validity of Caste and Exchange Theories, generally concluded that people marry interracially based on compatibility, love, and personal choice as opposed to caste-exchange.[25] These conclusions may lead one to erroneously believe that the intersecting effects of race, gender, and class are severely reduced or have no impact on the decisions whites make regarding the type of relationship partners they choose and that whites make decisions about marriage partners, whether interracial or intraracial, based solely on compatibility, mutual goals, respect, and love. Although race politics may not play out the way that Caste and Exchange Theories suggested, the role of race cannot be assumed to be null and void. The findings in this book reveal that race, intersected with gender and class, plays an integral role in the decisions white men make, as their deep frames of white-constructed knowledge about black female bodies discipline how they view black women and the relationships, or lack thereof, they seek with them.

Significantly, this research was completed after the historic election of President Barack Obama. Throughout the presidential campaign, particularly as it became clear that Obama could win the election and then after he accomplished the feat of victory, many news and political media outlets (and everyday people) proclaimed the start of a postracial society. Thus, these political pundits presented a distinct philosophical shift from the post–Jim Crow era's profession of a "colorblind" society to that of a "postracial" society, where race shifts from being unseen to nonexistent. The data in this book reveal that, indeed, intersecting race, gender, and class politics continue to be central components in society, and we are by no means colorblind or postracial. In fact, we will always have a racialized society, as long as the power of whites, particularly male elites, is normalized in the commonsense workings of society. And as long as the knowledge constructed by influential white men is normalized as superior within the deep frames of whites (and some people of color), discriminatory thoughts, perceptions, emotions, and actions along raced, gendered, and classed lines will continue to exist and go unchallenged.

Notes

1. Richard Dyer, *The Matter of Images: Essays on Representation*, 2nd ed. (New York: Routledge, 2002), p. 127.
2. Michel Foucault, *Discipline and Punish: The Birth of the Prison* (New York: Vintage Books, 1977), pp. 176–177.
3. Ibid.

4. Teun A. Van Dijk, *Discourse and Power* (New York: Palgrave, 2008).
5. See George Lakoff, *Thinking Points: Communicating Our American Values and Vision* (New York: Farrar, Straus, and Giroux, 2006).
6. Ibid.
7. Teun A. Van Dijk, *Racism and the Press* (New York: Routledge, 1991), p. 38.
8. bell hooks, *Black Looks: Race and Representation* (Boston: South End Press, 1992), p. 74.
9. Sharon M. Lee and Barry Edmonston, "New Marriages, New Families: U.S. Racial and Hispanic Intermarriage," *Population Reference Bureau* 60 (2005): 1–40.
10. Cited in Tatcho Mindiola Jr., Yolanda Flores Niemann, and Nestor Rodriguez, *Black-Brown: Relations and Stereotypes* (Austin: University of Texas Press, 2002), p. 30.
11. Mark E. Hill, "Skin Color and the Perception of Attractiveness Among African Americans: Does Gender Make a Difference?" *Social Psychology Quarterly* 65 (2002): 77–91.
12. DaTruthBeTold, "Monta Ellis Loves Wife, Life, Stephen Curry," *The Basketball Jones*. December 27, 2010 (retrieved April 4, 2011).
13. Joan Morgan, "When a Man Loves a Woman," *Essence*, November 2007, pp. 176–186.
14. Ibid.
15. Patricia H. Collins, *Black Sexual Politics: African Americans, Gender, and the New Racism* (New York: Routledge, 2005), p.194.
16. Dorothy Roberts, *Killing the Black Body: Race, Reproduction, and the Meaning of Liberty* (New York: Pantheon Books, 1997); Deborah G. White, *Ar'n't I a Woman? Female Slaves in the Plantation South* (New York: W.W. Norton and Company, 1985).
17. Roberts, *Killing the Black Body*.
18. Darlene C. Hines, *Hine Sight: Black Women and the Re-Construction of American History* (New York: Carlson Publishing, 1994), p. 37.
19. bell hooks, *Ain't I a Woman: Black Women and Feminism* (Boston: South End Press, 1981), p. 83.
20. Joe R. Feagin, *White Racial Frame* (New York: Routledge, 2009), p. 172.
21. Charisse Jones and Kumea Shorter-Gooden, *Shifting: The Double Lives of Black Women in America* (New York: HarperCollins, 2003), p. 61.
22. Ibid., p. 190.
23. Ibid.
24. Others are Joe R. Feagin and Eileen O'Brien, *White Men on Race: Power, Privilege, and the Shaping of Cultural Conscious* (Boston: Beacon Press, 2003); and Leslie Houts Picca and Joe R. Feagin,

Two-Faced Racism: Whites in the Backstage and Frontstage (New York: Routledge, 2007).

25. Michael J. Rosenfeld, "A Critique of Exchange Theory in Mate Selection," *American Journal of Sociology* 110 (2005): 1284–1325; George Yancey and Sherelyn Yancey, "Interracial Dating: Evidence from Personal Advertisements," *Journal of Family Studies* 19 (1998): 334–348; Kristyan M. Kouri and Marcia Lasswell, "Black-White Marriages: Social Change and Intergenerational Mobility," *Marriage and Family Review* 19 (1993): 241–255; Ernest Porterfield, "Black-American Intermarriage in the United States," *Marriage and Family Review* 5 (1978): 17–34.

References

Abramovitz, Mimi. *Regulating the Lives of Women: Social Welfare Policy from Colonial Times to Present*. Boston: South End Press, 1996.

Anderson, Margaret L., and Howard F. Taylor. *Sociology: Understanding a Diverse Society*. 4th ed. Belmont, CA: Thomson Wadsworth, 2008.

Austin, Regina. "Sapphire Bound." In *Critical Race Theory*, edited by K. Crenshaw, N. Gotanda, G. Peller, and K. Thomas, 426–437. New York: The New Press, 1995.

Bailey, Thomas P. *Race Orthodoxy in the South: And Other Aspects of the Negro Question*. New York: Neale Publishing Company, 1914.

Beauboeuf-Lafontant, Tamara. "Keeping Up Appearances, Getting Fed Up: The Embodiment of Strength among African American Women." *Feminism, Race, Transnationalism* 5 (2005): 104–123.

Bobo, Lawrence D. "Laissez-Faire Racism, Racial Inequality, and the Role of the Social Sciences." In *Rethinking the Color Line: Readings in Race and Ethnicity*, edited by C. A. Gallagher, 155–164. New York: McGraw-Hill, 2009.

Bonilla-Silva, Eduardo. "Rethinking Racism: Toward a Structural Interpretation." *American Sociological Review* 62 (1997): 465–480.

———. "From Bi-Racial to Tri-Racial: Towards a New System of Racial Stratification in the USA." *Ethnic and Racial Studies* 27 (2004): 931–950.

Bryman, Alan. *Social Research Methods*. 3rd ed. New York: Oxford University Press, 2008.

Chanter, Tina. *Gender: Key Concepts in Philosophy*. New York: Continuum, 2006.

Chou, Rosalind S., and Joe R. Feagin. *The Myth of the Model Minority: Asian Americans Facing Racism.* Boulder, CO: Paradigm Publishers, 2008.

Collins, Patricia H. *Black Feminist Thought: Knowledge, Consciousness, and the Politics of Empowerment.* 2nd ed. New York: Routledge, 2000.

———. *Black Sexual Politics: African Americans, Gender, and the New Racism.* New York: Routledge, 2005.

Cox, Oliver C. *Race: A Study in Social Dynamics.* New York: Monthly Review Press, 1948.

Craig, Maxine L. *Ain't I a Beauty Queen? Black Women, Beauty, and the Politics of Race.* New York: Oxford University Press, 2002.

Craigslist. "Factsheet." 2009. http://www.craigslist.org/about/factsheet (accessed March 30, 2009).

Crenshaw, Kimberle. "Race, Reform, and Retrenchment: Transformation and Legitimation in Antidiscrimination Law." In *Critical Race Theory*, edited by K. Crenshaw, N. Gotanda, G. Peller, and K. Thomas, 103–126. New York: The New Press, 1995.

Crowder, Kyle D., and Stewart E. Tolnay. "A New Marriage Squeeze for Black Women: The Role of Racial Intermarriage by Black Men." *Journal of Marriage and the Family* 62 (2000): 792–807.

Davis, Kingsley. "Intermarriage in Caste Society." *American Anthropologist* 43 (1941): 376–395.

DaTruthBeTold. "Monta Ellis Loves Wife, Life, Stephen Curry." *The Basketball Jones.* December 27, 2010. http://blogs.thescore.com/tbj/2010/10/14/monta-ellis-loves-wife-life-stephen-curry (accessed April 4, 2011).

Delgado, Richard. "Storytelling for Oppositionists and Others: A Plea for Narrative." In *Critical Race Theory: The Cutting Edge.* 2nd ed., edited by R. Delgado and J. Stefancic, 60–70. Philadelphia: Temple University Press, 2000.

Dyer, Richard. *The Matter of Images: Essays on Representation.* 2nd ed. New York: Routledge, 2002.

Ellis, Havelock. *Studies in the Psychology of Sex, Volume IV: Sexual Selection in Man: I. Taste, II. Smell, III. Hearing, IV. Vision.* Philadelphia, PA: Davis Co., 1927.

Encyclopedia Britannica, or a Dictionary of Arts, Sciences, and Literature. 3rd ed. London: Archibald Constable and Company, 1798.

Fausto-Sterling, A. "Gender, Race, and Nation: The Comparative Anatomy of 'Hottentot' Women in Europe, 1815–17. In

Skin Deep, Spirit Strong: The Black Female Body in American Culture, edited by K. Wallace-Sanders, 66–98. Ann Arbor: University of Michigan Press, 2002.

Feagin, Joe R. *Racist America: Roots, Current Realities, and Future Reparations*. New York: Routledge, 2000.

———. *Systemic Racism: A Theory of Oppression*. New York: Routledge, 2006.

———. *White Racial Frame*. New York: Routledge, 2009.

Feagin, Joe R., and Clairece B. Feagin. *Racial and Ethnic Relations*. 8th ed. Upper Saddle River, NJ: Pearson Prentice Hall, 2008.

Feagin, Joe R., and Eileen O'Brien. *White Men on Race: Power, Privilege, and the Shaping of Cultural Conscious*. Boston: Beacon Press, 2003.

Feliciano, Cynthia, Belinda Robnett, and Golnaz Komaie. "Gendered Racial Exclusion among White Internet Daters." *Social Science Research* 38 (2008): 39–54.

Foucault, Michel. *Discipline and Punish: The Birth of the Prison*. New York: Vintage Books, 1977.

Gilman, Sander L. *Difference and Pathology: Stereotypes of Sexuality, Race, and Madness*. Ithaca, NY: Cornell University Press, 1985.

Goff, Phillip A., Margaret A. Thomas, and Matthew C. Jackson. "'Ain't I a Woman?': Towards an Intersectional Approach to Person Perception and Group-Based Harms." *Sex Roles* 59 (2008): 392–403.

Guy-Sheftall, Beverly. "The Body Politic: Black Female Sexuality and the Nineteenth-Century Euro-American Imagination." In *Skin Deep, Spirit Strong: The Black Female Body in American Culture*, edited by K. Wallace-Sanders, 13–36. Ann Arbor: University of Michigan Press, 2002.

Graves, Joseph. "Interview with Joseph Graves Jr., Evolutionary Biologist." *Race the Power of an Illusion*. 2003. http://www.pbs.org/race/000_About/002_04-background-01-06.htm (accessed April 4, 2011).

Hammonds, Evelyn M. "Toward a Genealogy of Black Female Sexuality: The Problematic of Silence." In *Feminist Genealogies, Colonial Legacies, Democratic Futures*, edited by M. Jacqui Alexander and C. Mohanty, 170–182. New York: Routledge, 1997.

Harris, Cheryl I. "Whiteness as Property." In *Critical Race Theory*, edited by K. Crenshaw, N. Gotanda, G. Peller, and K. Thomas, 276–291. New York: The New Press, 1995.

Hatchett, Shirley, and Howard Schuman. "White Respondents and Race-of-Interviewer Effects." *Public Opinion Quarterly* 39 (1975): 523–528.

Haymes, Stephen N. "White Culture and the Politics of Racial Difference." In *Multicultural Education, Critical Pedagogy and the Politics of Difference*, edited by C. E. Sleeter and P. L. McLaren, 105–128. Albany: State University of New York Press, 1995.

———. *Race, Culture, and the City: A Pedagogy for Black Urban Struggle.* Albany: State University of New York Press, 1995.

Hill, Mark E. "Skin Color and the Perception of Attractiveness among African Americans: Does Gender Make a Difference?" *Social Psychology Quarterly* 65 (2002): 77–91.

Hines, Darlene C. *Hine Sight: Black Women and the Re-Construction of American History.* New York: Carlson Publishing, 1994.

hooks, bell. *Ain't I a Woman: Black Women and Feminism.* Boston: South End Press, 1981.

———. *Black Looks: Race and Representation.* Boston: South End Press, 1992.

Iceland, John, Daniel H. Weinberg, and Erika Steinmetz. *Racial and Ethnic Residential Segregation in the United States: 1980–2000.* Washington, DC: U.S. Government Printing Office, 2002.

James, Nalita, and Hugh Busher. "Credibility, Authenticity and Voice: Dilemmas in Online Interviewing." *Qualitative Research* 6 (2006): 403–420.

Jefferson, Thomas. *Notes on the State of Virginia*, edited by D. Waldstreicher. New York: Penguin Classics, [1785] 2002.

Jones, Charisse, and Kumea Shorter-Gooden. *Shifting: The Double Lives of Black Women in America.* New York: HarperCollins, 2003.

Jones, James M., and Robert T. Carter. "Racism and White Racial Identity: Merging Realities." In *Impacts of Racism on White Americans.* 2nd ed., edited by B. P. Bowser and R. G. Hunt, 1–23. Thousand Oaks, CA: Sage Publications, Inc., 1996.

Kapsalis, Terri. "Mastering the Female Pelvis: Race and the Tools of Reproduction." In *Skin Deep, Spirit Strong: The Black Female Body in American Culture*, edited by K. Wallace-Sanders, 263–300. Ann Arbor: University of Michigan Press, 2002.

Kellner, Peter. "Can Online Polls Produce Accurate Findings?" *International Journal of Market Research* 46 (2004): 1.

Kouri, Kristyan M., and Marcia Lasswell. "Black-White Marriages: Social Change and Intergenerational Mobility." *Marriage and Family Review* 19 (1993): 241–255.

Lakoff, George. *Don't Think of an Elephant! Know Your Values and Frame the Debate.* White River Junction, VT: Chelsea Green Publishing Company, 2004.

———. *Whose Freedom? The Battle over America's Most Important Idea.* New York: Farrar, Straus, and Giroux, 2006.

———. *Thinking Points: Communicating Our American Values and Vision.* New York: Farrar, Straus, and Giroux, 2006.

———. *The Political Mind: Why You Can't Understand 21st Century American Politics with an 18th Century Brain.* New York: Penguin Group, 2008.

Latifah, Queen. "U.N.I.T.Y." *Black Reign.* 1993.

Lee, Sharon M., and Barry Edmonston. "New Marriages, New Families: U.S. Racial and Hispanic Intermarriage." *Population Reference Bureau* 60 (2005): 1–40.

Long, Edward. *The History of Jamaica, or, General Survey of the Antient and Modern State of that Island: With Reflections on Its Situation, Settlements, Inhabitants, Climate, Products, Commerce, Laws, and Government.* London: T. Lowndes, 1774.

Lowrey, Ying. *Minorities in Business: A Demographic Review of Minority Business Ownership.* Washington, DC: U.S. Small Business Research Administration, 2007.

McCabe, Sean E. "Comparison of Mail and Web Surveys in Collecting Illicit Drug Use Data: A Randomized Experiment." *Journal of Drug Education* 34 (2004): 61–73.

McKinney, Karyn D. *Being White: Stories of Race and Racism.* New York: Routledge, 2005.

McLaren, Peter L. *Critical Pedagogy and Predatory Culture: Oppositional Politics in a Post Modern Era.* New York: Routledge, 1995.

Merton, Robert K. "Interracial Marriage and the Social Structure: Fact and Theory." *Psychiatry* 4 (1941): 361–374.

Mindiola, Tatcho, Jr., Yolando F. Niemann, and Nestor Rodriguez. *Black-Brown Relations and Stereotypes.* Austin: University of Texas Press, 2002.

Morgan, Jennifer L. "'Some Could Suckle over Their Shoulder': Male Travelers, Female Bodies, and the Gendering of Racial Ideology, 1500–1770." In *Skin Deep, Spirit Strong: The Black Female Body in American Culture,* edited by K. Wallace-Sanders, 37–65. Ann Arbor: University of Michigan Press, 2002.

Morgan, Joan. "When a Man Loves a Woman." *Essence,* November 2007: 176–186.

Moynihan, Daniel. *The Negro Family: The Case for National Action.* Washington, DC: U.S. Government Printing Office, 1965.

Murthy, Dhiraj. "Digital Ethnography: An Examination of the Use of New Technologies for Social Research." *Sociology* 42 (2008): 837–855.

Newport, Frank. "Little 'Obama Effect' on Views about Race Relations." Gallup, October 29, 2009. http://www.gallup.com/poll/123944/Little-Obama-Effect-Views-Race-Relations.aspx (accessed March 31, 2011).

Northup, Solomon. *Twelve Years a Slave*. New York: Miller, Orton, and Mulligan, 1855.

Omi, Michael, and Howard Winant. *Racial Formation in the United States*. 2nd ed. New York: Routledge, 1994.

Phua, Voon C., and Gayle Kaufman. "The Crossroads of Race and Sexuality: Date Selection among Men in Internet 'Personal' Ads." *Journal of Family Issues* 24 (2005): 981–994.

Picca, Leslie H., and Joe R. Feagin. *Two-Faced Racism: Whites in the Backstage and Frontstage*. New York: Routledge, 2007.

Porterfield, Ernest. "Black-American Intermarriage in the United States." *Marriage and Family Review* 5 (1978): 17–34.

Qian, Zhenchao, and Daniel T. Litcher. "Social Boundaries and Marital Assimilation: Interpreting Trends in Racial and Ethnic Intermarriage." *American Sociological Review* 72 (2007): 68–94.

Reyes, Robert Paul. "William Bennett: Abort Black Babies to Reduce Crime." *American Chronicle*, October 1, 2005. http://www.americanchronicle.com/articles/view/2685 (accessed April 2, 2011).

Roberts, Dorothy. *Killing the Black Body: Race, Reproduction, and the Meaning of Liberty*. New York: Pantheon Books, 1997.

Rosenfeld, Michael J. "A Critique of Exchange Theory in Mate Selection." *American Journal of Sociology* 110 (2005): 1284–1325.

Shapiro, Thomas. *The Hidden Cost of Being African American: How Wealth Perpetuates Inequality*. New York: Oxford University Press, 2004.

Sharpley-Whiting, Tracy D. *Sexualized Savages, Primal Fears, and Primitive Narratives in French*. Durham, NC: Duke University Press, 1999.

Sudman, Seymour, and Norman M. Bradburn. *Asking Questions: A Practical Guide to Questionnaire Design*. San Francisco: Josey-Bass, 1982.

Taylor, Humphrey. "Does Internet Research Work? Comparing Electronic Survey Results with Telephone Surveys." *International Journal of Market Research* 42, 1 (2000): 51–63.

Thomas, Susan L. "Race, Gender, and Welfare Reform: The Antinatalist Response." *Journal of Black Studies* 28 (1998): 419–446.

U.S. Bureau of the Census. *Interracial Married Couples: 1980 to 2002.* Washington, DC: U.S. Government Printing Office, 2004.

Van Dijk, Teun A. *Racism and the Press.* New York: Routledge, 1991.

———. *Discourse and Power.* New York: Palgrave, 2008.

Vera, Hernan, and Andrew M. Gordon. *Screen Saviors: Hollywood Fictions of Whiteness.* Lanham, MD: Rowman and Littlefield Publishers, Inc., 2003.

Victoria's Secret. "Denim Sale." *Victoria's Secret,* December 2008: 28.

White, Deborah G. *Ar'n't I a Woman? Female Slaves in the Plantation South.* New York: W.W. Norton and Company, 1985.

Yancey, George. "Homogamy Over the Net: Using Internet Advertisements to Discover Who Interracially Dates." *Journal of Social and Personal Relationships* 24 (2007): 913–930.

Yancey, George, and Sherelyn Yancey. "Interracial Dating: Evidence from Personal Advertisements." *Journal of Family Studies* 19 (1998): 334–348.

Index

Ain't I a Beauty Queen? Black Women, Beauty, and the Politics of Race (Craig), 42–43
Animalism, 13–17, 21, 100–101
Anti-women, black women as, 83–85, 97, 118–119
Apes, 15
Asian Americans, 39, 42, 114
Assimilation, 62–71
Athletes, professional, 115–117

Baartman, Saartjie, 12–13, 51–52
Backstage racism, 5–6
Bailey, Thomas Pierce, 16
Basketball, professional, 115–117
Beauty: black women with "black" features, 44–46; black women's buttocks, 49–50; discourse of comparison, 53–57; multiracial women, 42–43; white construction of, 14–15, 97; "white" features in black women, 40–41
Bestiality, 13–14
Beyoncé, 44, 51, 54
Biological inferiority of blacks, 21–22, 88–90
Bitchiness, 99–100
Black as racial term, 9–10

Black Looks: Race and Representation (hooks), 113
Black men: black men-white women relationships, 97–99; intermarriage rate, 6–7, 96–100; intraracial relationships, 94–95
Black other, 104
Blackness: normalization of whiteness, 37–39
Body image, 1–2
Buffon, Georges-Louis, 15
Burdensome usurper, 71–78
Business ownership, 77
Buttocks, 48–52, 55, 66, 102, 104

Caste Theory, 3, 121
Charpy, Adrian, 15–16
Children and childbearing: black women as baby machines, 19–20; black women's reproduction as threat, 20; childbearing, 14; as deterrent to interracial marriage, 102; "good" and "bad" black women, 72–73; slave women protecting children, 117–118
Choose Me (film), 113
Class: burdensome usurpers and hardworking

132

Index **133**

bootstrappers, 71–78; Caste and Exchange Theories of interracial marriage, 3–4; classed image of black women as marriage partners, 63–64; cultural depravity theory, 22–23; history of discrimination, 78–80; interracial marriage rate, 7–8; intersection with race and gender, 4–5; mammy caricature, 17–18; normalizing white culture, 65; research questions, 29; roots of white hegemony, 59–60; social construction of culture and identity, 9–11; welfare queens, 20, 72, 75–76, 83; white men's narratives of black women, 87; white-defined culture, 60–61
Clinton, Bill, 35n79
Cognitive skills, deep frame operating from, 9
Colorblind ideology: black cultural depravity, 22–23; describing physical attraction to black women, 40; interracial marriage perceptions, 4; political shifts, 122; research methodology, 25–27; white men's narratives of black women, 88
Commoditization: of black women's buttocks, 49–50; of black women's sexuality, 102–104, 119–120; controlling perception of beauty, 57; exotification by white culture, 60–61; of hip hop, 78
Comparisons. *See* Discourse of comparisons

Constructing black women, 113–114
Coping skills of black women, 120–121
Corruption, racial, 69
Counter-frame, 119
Craig, Maxine Leeds, 42–43
Craigslist, 36n91
Cultural depravity, 22–23, 63
Cultural deprivation, 59
Cultural inferiority, 110–112
Culture: black culture and white assimilation, 62–71; burdensome usurpers and hardworking bootstrappers, 71–78; learning deep frames, 23–25; perceived ineptness of black culture, 78–80; white culture as the normative standard, 59–61, 64–71
Culture of poverty, 69
Cuvier, Georges, 13

Dating: cultural difference, 61; disciplinary power of deep frames, 112; downplaying race, gender, and class, 4; exclusion of black women, 7–8, 40; gendered racial exclusion in Internet dating, 31n6; research questions, 28–30; respondents' experiences with black women, 28(table); social pressure framing interracial dating, 46, 56–57, 97–98; types of dating relationships with black women, 29(table)
Deep frame: black women with "black" features, 44; contemporary shifts in, 21–23; defining, 2;

Deep frame (continued): disciplinary power of, 107–112; early framing of black women, 12–17; embedded, 24–25; learning, 23–25; mammy construction, 17–18; normalization of whiteness, 37–39; white racial frame, 32n28. *See also* Social construction
Derogatory terms for black women, 120
Discourse of comparisons: normalization of white women, 38–39; perceived vulgarity of black women, 89–90; physical appearance, 53–57; "white" features in black women, 40–41
Discrimination: education for blacks, 76–77; residential spaces, 76–77; understanding the history of, 78–80. *See also* Racism
Disease, 88–89
Dissemblance, culture of, 118
Dominant culture: creating its own narrative, 83; power structures shaping group perceptions, 111; whiteness as normative standard, 60–61
Domineering black women, 91–92, 99–100, 102

Education: hardworking bootstrappers, 75–76; history of racial discrimination, 79–80; interracial marriage rate, 7; normalizing white culture and values, 66–67; perception of black families' lack of interest in, 94; stereotypical view of black women, 1–2; white assimilation, 62–63; white-dominated culture, 60
Elder, Glen, 3
Ellis, Havelock, 97
Emasculating matriarchs perspective, 18–19
Embedded deep frames, 24–25
Employment: entrepreneurial endeavors, 77; strong black matriarchs construction, 18–19; whites' perceptions of blacks' opportunities, 5
Encyclopedia Britannica, 10
Entrepreneurial endeavors, 77
European males: constructing knowledge and meaning, 113; controlling hegemonic notions of culture, 59–60; early framing of black women, 12–17; learning deep frames, 23–25; origins of deep frames, 9–10; strong black matriarchs, 18–19; white-defined beauty, 97; white-defined culture, 60–61
Exchange Theory, 3, 121
Exclusion of black women, 6–8, 40
Exotification of black sexuality and culture, 48–49, 55–56, 61, 101–103
Eye color, 51

Family: discouraging interracial dating, 46, 56–57, 97–98; gendered roles in black families, 92–93; respondents' experiences with black community, 28(table); white assimilation, 62–63
Fashion, 49, 74

Index

Femininity: black women with "black" features, 44; black women's exclusion from, 111–112; black women's strength, 95; expectation of black women's adaptation to white culture, 70; perception of black women's lack of, 46–48, 88, 93; unwantedness of black women, 99
Foreign-born blacks, 6, 68, 87
Foster, Tameka, 116
Foucault, Michel, 37(quote), 38, 65, 107
Friends: discouraging interracial dating, 46; respondents' experiences with black women, 28(table)
Frontstage performances, 5–6, 26

Gender: Caste and Exchange Theories of interracial marriage, 3–4; interracial Internet dating preferences, 8; intersection with class and race, 4–5; research questions, 29
Gender roles, traditional, 118
Generational welfare regime, 76
Genitalia, 12–13, 16, 48–53
Genocide, 24
Ghetto class, 65, 72–73
Goffman, Erving, 5

Hair color, texture, and style, 43, 45, 51, 54, 64, 115–116; shifting, 120
Half-caste individuals, 97
Hardworking bootstrapper, 71–78
Haymes, Stephen, 65
Heterotoptas, 65

Hierarchy, racial, 10–11, 37–38, 110
Hines, Darlene Clark, 118
Hip hop, 78, 120
The History of Jamaica (Long), 14
HIV/AIDS, 88–89
Hooks, bell [suppress], 17, 103, 113, 118
Hottentot (Khoikhoi group), 12–13
Housing discrimination, 79–80
Human rights movement, 21
Hypertrophy of the labia, 52–53

Identity: black culture as form of resistance, 68–69, 74–75; deep frames representing, 9; history of racial discrimination against black women, 80; multiracial, 41–43, 54; names and fashion, 73–74
Illegitimate births, 20
Imitation of Life (film), 113
Immigrants, 70–71
Income inequality, 79–80
Intellectual inferiority, perception of, 69
Intelligence: "white" features in black women, 41–42
Intermarriage. *See* Marriage, interracial
Internet: gendered racial exclusion in Internet dating, 31n6; online questionnaires, 25–27; racial preferences on dating sites, 8; research methodology, 121

Jefferson, Thomas, 11–12, 15, 61, 86
Jim Crow era, 11, 21

Index

Jokes and epithets, racial, 26
Jolly, Wilbur, 20

Keys, Alicia, 41, 51, 54
Khoikhoi women,
    12–13, 16, 51–52

Labia, hypertrophy
    of the, 52–53
Language and dominant
    culture, 60
Latinos/Latinas, 39, 54–55, 114
Laziness, perception
    of, 77, 85–86
Legislation: anti-interracial
    marriage law, 3
Leprosy, 88–89
Liberty, justice, and
    equality for all, 24
Lips, 13, 15, 40, 42, 52,
    55, 57, 102–104
Living Single (television
    program), 120
Long, Edward, 14–15

Mammy caricature, 17–18
Marriage, interracial: black
    men and white women,
    96–100; black women
    as domineering, 91–92;
    blaming the victim, 78;
    Caste Theory and Exchange
    Theory, 3–4; decision-making
    factors for white men,
    121–122; downplaying race,
    gender, and class, 4–5;
    low rate of black women's
    marriage, 113–114; men's
    negative perception of,
    86; professional athletes,
    115–116; racist view of
    conditions for, 89; statistics
    on black women and women
    of color, 6–7; unwantedness
    of black women, 99–100;
    white assimilation, 63
Masculinity, 46–48
Matriarch construction,
    18–19, 92–93
Media: dominant white
    culture, 77; learning deep
    frames, 24; limited positive
    images of black women,
    64; shaping perception of
    black women, 108–109
Middle-class black
    women, 118–119
Moral inferiority,
    perception of, 69, 85
Mothers' pensions, 35n80
Moynihan, Daniel, 18, 92
Mulatto identity, 42
Multiracial identity, 41–43, 54

Names, 72, 74–75
Narratives: black men-white
    women relationships, 96–100;
    black women as anti-
    women, 83–84; burdensome
    usurper and hardworking
    bootstrapper, 71–78; cultural
    difference, 61; domineering
    black women, 91–92; function
    of, 9; racial and cultural
    identity, 70–71; strength of
    black women, 90–91; taboo
    sex with black women,
    103–104; white men's stories
    of black women, 84–90
National Basketball Association
    (NBA) players, 115–117
Native Americans, 39, 114
Negro as terminology, 10
*The Negro Family: The
    Case for National Action*
    (Moynihan), 92
Normalization: of beauty, 51–52;
    of white beauty, 64–71,

99; of white culture, 62, 78–80; of whiteness, 37–39
Norplant, 20
Notes on the State of Virginia (Jefferson), 11–12, 15, 86

Obama, Barack, 122
Oppositional discourse, 53–57
Oppression: black women's resistance to, 117–118; blaming the victim, 75

Parity, 59
Pathologizing black women, 51–53, 113
Patriarchal norms of femininity, 95
Personal hygiene, 87–88, 101
Personal Responsibility and Work Reconciliation Act, 35n79
Phallus glorification, 78
Physical appearance of black women: the black sexual body, 48–53; black women as sexual objects, 102–103; black women with "black" features, 44–53; black women with "white" features, 39–44; discourse of comparison, 53–57; European males' perceptions, 14–15; "good" and "bad" black women, 72; normalization of whiteness, 37–39; skin color determining attractiveness, 114; white culture and assimilation, 64; white men's narratives, 85–88
Political correctness: black cultural depravity, 22–23; postracial society, 122
Poverty: blaming the victim, 75; cultural deprivation, 61; culture of, 69, 73–74; as Negro problem, 20; racializing residential spaces, 67
Power, 107–112
Pressures on black women, 93–94
Primates, white men's view of black women as, 13, 15, 89
Prostitution, 15, 100, 102

Quadroons, 42
Queen Latifah, 119–120

Race: black race as corrupt, 69; black women as anti-women, 84–85; Caste and Exchange Theories of interracial marriage, 3–4; choosing marriage partners, 121–122; demonizing black culture, 62; educating black women, 77; intersection with class and gender, 4–5; normalization of whiteness, 37–39; research questions, 29; social construction of culture and identity, 9–11
Race, Culture, and the City (Haymes), 65
Race Orthodoxy in the South and Other Aspects of the Negro Question (Bailey), 16
Racialization of social spaces, 64–67
Racism: backstage, 5–6; biological inferiority of blacks, 21–22; black women's coping skills, 120; cultural depravity construct, 22–23
Rape, 16–17
Raymond, Usher, 116
Reagan, Ronald, 20–21, 74
Real estate discrimination, 67
Redlining, 67

Relationships, shifting, 120
Reproduction. *See* Children and childbearing
Research methodology, 25–30, 28(table)–29(table)
Residential spaces, 64–67, 76–77
Resistance, black women's, 116–121

Segregated neighborhoods, 67, 76–77
Service-sector jobs, 85
Sexual attraction. *See* Physical appearance
Sexual encounters with black women, 68, 87, 92, 97–98, 100–101, 103–104
Sexual objects, black women as, 100–104, 112
Sexual orientation: racial preferences on dating sites, 8
Sexuality: the black sexual body, 48–53; black women as anti-women, 83–84; black women's resistance to sexualization, 118–121; early exhibits of "primitive" women, 12–13; sexual addiction, 100; sexual deviance, 15–16, 86, 113; sexual fantasies, 101; white construction of beauty, 15; white men's narratives of black women's inferiority, 88–89; white men's perceptions of black women, 100–104
Sexually transmitted disease, 88–89
Shifting, 120–121
Side shows, 12–13
Single mothers, 18–19, 95, 116
Skin color, 41, 43, 45, 54, 115–116

Slavery: black women as sex slaves, 15; black women's childbearing, 19; black women's resistance, 117–118; desirability of mulattos and quadroons, 42; mammy caricature, 17–18; rape and, 16–17; social construction of culture and identity, 9–10; strength of black women, 95; strong black matriarchs, 18
Small Business Administration Office of Advocacy Report, 77
Social construction: baby machines and welfare queens, 20–21; early framing of black women, 12–17; of knowledge, 9–10; strong black matriarchs, 18–19
Steatopygia, 51–52
Stereotypes: black men-white women relationships, 98; black women as anti-women, 83–84; exclusion of black women as partners, 6–8; "good" and "bad" black women, 72; Jeffersonian view of blacks, 11–12; "Negroes," 10
Sterilization, forced, 20
Strength of black women, 90, 94–95
Studies in the Psychology of Sex (Ellis), 97
Suburbia, 64–67
Superiority of white men, 101
Syphilis, 88–89

Taboo sex, 103–104
Traits of black women, 90–91, 93
Travelers and tourists: early framing of black women, 12–14
Turnipseed, Edward, 52–53

Index

"U.N.I.T.Y." (song), 120
Unwanted woman, black women as, 98–104, 110
Uplift jeans, 49

Vaginas, 52–53
Values: "good" and "bad" black women, 72

Welfare: black women as welfare queens, 19–21, 71–73, 75–76, 83; blaming the victim, 74–76; reforms, 35n79, 76; white men's perception of black women, 63–64
White women: interracial marriage rate, 7

White-defined culture, 60–61
Whiteness: as basis for healthy relationships, 70; inherent power, 107–108; normalization of, 37–39; white assimilation, 62–71; white construction of beauty, 14–15, 97; white culture as the normative standard, 59–60, 64–71; white racial frame, 9–10, 32n28
Widows and children, welfare and, 21
Work ethic: burdensome usurpers and hardworking bootstrappers, 71–78; cultural depravity argument, 22

◆

About the Author

Brittany C. Slatton earned her doctorate from Texas A&M University, College Station, and is Assistant Professor of Sociology at Texas Southern University. Her work examines the intersections of race, gender, class, and sexuality, and relationship dynamics.